You Want Me to Do What?

You Want Me to Do What?

Get Off Your Blessed Assurance and Do Something!

Michael Youssef, PhD

New York   Boston   Nashville

FaithWords
Hachette Book Group
237 Park Avenue
New York, NY 10017

Visit our Web site at www.faithwords.com.

Printed in the United States of America

First Edition: March 2009
10 9 8 7 6 5 4 3 2 1

FaithWords is a division of Hachette Book Group, Inc.
The FaithWords name and logo are trademarks of Hachette Book Group, Inc.

Library of Congress Cataloging-in-Publication Data

Youssef, Michael.
   You want me to do what? : get off your blessed assurance and do something! / Michael Youssef. — 1st ed.
      p. cm.
   ISBN-13: 978-0-446-57958-2
   1. Bible. O.T. Joshua—Criticism, interpretation, etc. I. Title.
   BS1295.52.Y68 2009
   222'.026—dc22

                                                        2008022341

To the faithful members of The Church of The Apostles in Atlanta, Georgia, with thanksgiving and deep appreciation . . . for their enthusiastic response to the message of this book and starting a citywide movement called "ApostlesLife."

CONTENTS

Overview: Trembling Heroes   ix

1 **You Want Me to Step Up?**   1
   Joshua 1

2 **You Want Me to Go into Enemy Territory?**   27
   Joshua 2

3 **You Want Me to Cross the River of Impossibility?**   44
   Joshua 3–4

4 **You Want Me to Yield?**   60
   Joshua 5

5 **You Want Me to Get with the Program?**   75
   Joshua 6

6 **You Want Me to Learn from My Mistakes?**   91
   Joshua 7–8

7 **You Want Me to Learn to Pray for Discernment?**   112
   Joshua 9

8   *You Want Me to Claim the Total Victory?*   130
      Joshua 10–12

9   *You Want Me to Trust in the Cosmic Real Estate Developer?*   149
      Joshua 13–17

10 *You Want Me to Claim My Inheritance?*   165
      Joshua 18–19

11 *You Want Me to Be a Runner to the City of Refuge?*   183
      Joshua 20

12 *You Want Me to Tell the Story?*   196
      Joshua 21–24

    Notes   217

    About the Author   225

Overview

Trembling Heroes

Joshua was a towering hero of the Old Testament.

And Joshua was an ordinary human being like you and me.

Can both of those statements be true? Absolutely! We need to rid ourselves of this notion that the people in the Bible were somehow larger-than-life. Those ancient heroes like Moses, Joshua, Samuel, David, Peter, and Paul were just human beings, made of the same human clay that you and I are—no more and no less.

After all, what is a hero? A hero is just an ordinary person who takes on an extraordinary challenge, ignores his pounding heart and knocking knees, and does what must be done. If we could truly grasp the fact that our "Bible heroes" are no different from us, our understanding of Scripture would be transformed.

The Bible heroes we view as "fearless" were actually shaking in their sandals. These people we view as "giants of the faith" were actually riddled with questions and doubts. Yet, in spite of their doubts and fears, they followed God, they carried out the mission He gave them, and God used them in mighty ways.

And God hasn't changed. He still works through flawed, fallible, fearful human beings like you and me.

You may have felt God calling you to attempt some "impossible" task. Perhaps He wants you to forgive your worst enemy. Or start a ministry to children in your neighborhood. Or begin a lunch-hour Bible study at your office. Or start a visitation ministry in a nearby prison. Or reach out with the love of Christ to the homeless people in your community. Or share the good news of the gospel with someone who has a difficult and intimidating personality.

And even though you feel God calling you and tugging at you, something within you pulls back and says, "Lord, You want me to do *what*?"

I know that feeling myself. I've been there many times. And that's why I've written this book. My friend, I want you to know that God understands your reluctance and your self-doubt. That's why, in His Word, the Lord has given us so many stories of men and women, common folk like you and me, who answered God's call to dare great things for Him.

One of those people was the Old Testament leader Joshua. As you and I explore his life together, we will see a man who was just like us in so many ways. Again and again, God issued a challenge to Joshua, and Joshua's initial response was just like ours: "You want me to do *what*?"

In the pages to come, you and I will discover together how Joshua moved beyond his initial fears and reluctance to a place of faith, confidence, and obedience. We'll learn how

Joshua was able to achieve astonishing things for God. Most important, we'll discover how to apply the lessons of Joshua's story to our own lives.

Let's begin by taking a closer look at this flesh-and-blood man named Joshua.

Counsel and Comfort for Impossible Challenges

We first find Joshua mentioned in Exodus and Numbers, where he is mentored by Moses and sent out as one of twelve spies to explore the land of Canaan in preparation for the conquest of that land. He later becomes the leader of the nation of Israel in the book of Joshua. In that account, Joshua, the son of Nun, of the tribe of Ephraim, is handpicked by God Himself to assume the mantle of leadership after the death of Moses. As commander of the army of Israel, Joshua leads his people in their military conquest of the promised land.

The events of the book of Joshua are hinted at in nonbiblical records, such as the Amarna Letters, a collection of ancient clay tablets that were found at Amarna in Upper Egypt. These ancient records include appeals by Canaanite kings for military assistance from Egypt because of an invasion by the Hapiru people, described as fierce nomadic tribes who invaded the land of Canaan. Some archaeologists and historians have suggested that Hapiru might be a corrupted form of the word *Hebrew.*

The book of Joshua recounts the conquest of the heavily fortified city of Jericho, followed by both failure and success at Ai, the dramatic and supernaturally aided battles at Gibeon and at the Waters of Mermon, and more. By the end of the book, Joshua—who was born a slave in the land of Egypt—has completed the mission the Lord set before him and is laid to rest at the age of 110.

It's a thrilling chronicle of amazing events, and the story of Joshua has much to teach us about how we can live victorious lives today, in the twenty-first century. Again and again, at every crossroads in Joshua's journey of faith, God calls Joshua and the nation of Israel to accept a seemingly impossible challenge. Again and again, Joshua faces a moment where he seems to look heavenward and ask, "You want me to do *what*?"

And the choice Joshua makes at each of those critical moments is profoundly instructive for our lives. The principles of faith and obedience that guided Joshua are the very same principles that will guide you and me to a more fruitful and victorious Christian life. Here is counsel for those times in our lives when we face an overwhelming crisis or an impossible challenge. Here is comfort and wisdom for those moments when we look to God and ask—

"You want me to do *what*?"

You
Want
Me to Do
What?

1

You Want Me to Step Up?

Joshua 1

Sergeant James Allen Ward was just twenty-two years old when he was called upon to do the impossible.

During World War II, Sergeant Ward flew with the Seventy-fifth New Zealand Squadron of the Royal Air Force. He had recently been assigned as copilot aboard a Vickers Wellington bomber based in southeastern England and was still gaining experience piloting the twin-engine medium bomber.

On July 7, 1941, Sergeant Ward and his fellow crewmen carried out a daring nighttime bombing mission over Münster, Germany. Returning from the successful raid, the bomber was thirteen thousand feet over Holland when it was attacked by a German Messerschmitt Bf 110 nightfighter. The enemy plane approached within mere yards of the tail of the RAF bomber, its nose cannons and machine guns blazing.

The bomber's rear gun turret was blasted to shreds by the gunfire. The tailgunner, Sgt. A. J. R. Box, was grievously wounded in the leg, but he fought back, spraying the attacking aircraft with machine-gun fire. The Messerschmitt fell away and spiraled toward the earth—but its incendiary bullets had already pierced the RAF bomber's wing near the starboard engine, severing a fuel line and setting the wing on fire.

Up in the cockpit of the bomber, Capt. Ben Widdowson saw the blazing wing and turned to his copilot, Sgt. James Allen Ward. "You've got to put that fire out," Widdowson said.

Hearing those words, Sergeant Ward must have thought, *You want me to do* what? How was he supposed to put out a fire on the starboard engine? But Sergeant Ward knew he had to think of something—fast. If the fire spread and engulfed the wing, the plane would go down over Nazi-occupied Holland. Even if the crew bailed out safely, they would be captured and end up in a Nazi prison camp.

As Captain Widdowson throttled back and slowed the plane to just over a hundred miles per hour, Sergeant Ward and another crewman cut a hole in the side of the plane and tried to smother the flames with fire extinguishers. Unfortunately, the spray from the extinguishers was dispersed by the airplane's slipstream before it could reach the flames. Sergeant Ward went back to the cockpit and reported the failure to the pilot.

"Then prepare the crew to bail out," Captain Widdowson said.

Through the Astro-Hatch

Sergeant Ward quickly considered the prospect of a life in a Nazi prison camp. "There's got to be something we can do," he said.

Captain Widdowson said, "You could go out on the wing and smother the fire."

Again, Sergeant Ward must have thought, *You want me to do* what? He was a copilot, not a wing-walking stuntman! But he looked out the window at the flaming starboard engine and remembered all the grisly tales he had heard about Nazi prison camps—

"I'll do it," he said.

Sergeant Ward and several crewmen took a rope from the inflatable life raft and tied one end around his waist while securing the other end to the airframe. Then they popped open the astro-hatch, a small Plexiglas dome on top of the plane used to observe the stars in celestial navigation. The opening was narrow—and for a few tense moments it seemed that Sergeant Ward was wedged there, unable to move in either direction. Fighting down feelings of panic, he squeezed through the astro-hatch. The crewmen passed a parachute through the hole, and he strapped it on while clinging to the top of the plane. Then the crewmen handed him a sheet of canvas to use in smothering the flames.

The skin of the Vickers Wellington bomber was made of Irish linen stretched over the aircraft's framework and lacquered to make it durable. Sergeant Ward used his fists and boots to punch holes in the lacquer-stiffened fabric to form handholds and footholds. Then, as the crewmen payed out the rope, Sergeant Ward clambered down to the wing.

He punched more holes in the fabric of the wing and slowly made his way toward the burning engine. All the while, the airflow buffeted him and tried to pry him from the wing. As he approached the engine, the heat from the flames threatened to force him back.

Sergeant Ward held the canvas in front of him and shoved it into the flame-spewing hole at the rear of the engine housing. Burning fuel continued to spray out around the edges of the canvas, and the airman feared that the canvas itself would ignite—

Then the flames went out.

Sergeant Ward tried to stuff the canvas into the hole in hopes of stanching the flow of petrol from the severed fuel line, but as soon as he took his hand away, the canvas blew off and was lost. The fuel continued to leak, but the fire was out and the plane was saved.

Moving hand over hand as his fellow crewmen pulled in the rope, Sergeant Ward made his way back across the wing, up the side of the plane, and back through the narrow astro-hatch.

A Hero with Knocking Knees

As the plane approached the landing field, nearly six hours after taking off on its perilous journey, Captain Widdowson discovered that the flaps—which slow the plane and maintain lift during landings—could not be lowered. The controls had apparently been damaged by the German airplane's guns. So Widdowson had to bring the plane down too fast, hoping to stop the plane safely by applying the wheel brakes. Then, as the plane touched down and rolled down the airstrip, Widdowson discovered he had no brakes.

The bomber rolled off the end of the airstrip and plowed through a hedge and a barbed-wire fence. The impact shattered the airplane—but the crew, including Sergeant Ward, emerged from the wreckage unhurt. A month later, Sgt. James Allen Ward was awarded the Victoria Cross—the nation's highest honor for courage in the face of the enemy. It was the first Victoria Cross ever awarded to a New Zealander.

The British prime minister, Winston Churchill, summoned Sergeant Ward to No. 10 Downing Street to commend the young man for his heroism. As Sergeant Ward came into the prime minister's office, Churchill tried to chat with him about his experience—but the young man couldn't answer any of the prime minister's questions. The airman's knees knocked, his hands shook, and he could not come up with a single word of reply. Churchill was amazed. This brave young airman had crawled across the burning wing of an airplane at thirteen thousand feet—yet he was terrified to speak to the British prime minister!

"Son," Churchill said, "you must feel very humble and awkward to be in my presence."

Sergeant Ward gulped, nodded, and managed to say, "Yes, sir."

"Then you can imagine," Churchill said, "how humble and awkward I feel in yours."[1]

Sergeant James Allen Ward was a hero—even to the head of state of Great Britain—because he accepted the "impossible" assignment and acted obediently and courageously in the moment of crisis. Yes, he had his moment of doubt, his moment of thinking, *You want me to do* what?

But then he accepted the challenge, tackled the "impossible" task, and enabled the crew of his crippled aircraft to safely reach home.

You and I will probably never be called upon to crawl onto a flaming airplane wing. But we will be called to face crises and challenges for the sake of our Lord. We will be called upon to dare and to risk—and possibly to fail in the attempt.

We will confront challenges that, to us, may seem every bit as impossible as the crisis Sergeant Ward faced.

And at such moments, we will turn our eyes toward heaven and say to God, "You want me to do *what?*" That is the moment we must make a choice: Do we trust God to strengthen us and see us through this challenge, win or lose, live or die? Or will we shrink back in fear and unbelief, rejecting God's will for our lives?

It's normal to feel reluctant in the face of a great challenge. But after that moment of initial reluctance and inner questioning, we must come to a place of obedience. That is the example set for us by Sergeant Ward.

And that, as we are about to see, was the response of Joshua when God commanded, "Step up!"

"Be Strong and Courageous!"

The book of Joshua opens with these words:

After the death of Moses the servant of the LORD, the LORD said to Joshua son of Nun, Moses' aide: "Moses my servant is dead. Now then, you and all these people, get ready to cross the Jordan River into the land I am about to give to them—to the Israelites. I will give you every place where you set your foot, as I promised Moses. Your territory will extend from the desert to Lebanon, and from the great river, the Euphrates—all the Hittite country—to the Great Sea on the west. No one will be able to stand up against you all the days of your life. As I was with Moses, so I will be with you; I will never leave you nor forsake you."

(Josh. 1:1–5)

As the book of Joshua opens, Moses is dead. So God goes to Joshua, the faithful right-hand man of Moses, and tells him, in effect, "Joshua, I want you to *step up*! I want you to lead My people into the land I have given them."

The Scripture text does not tell us in so many words that Joshua felt any reluctance in the face of God's command. But I believe there are strong hints that Joshua doubted he was up to the task God had set before him. In this passage, God clearly finds it necessary to build up Joshua's courage and confidence to step up to this challenge.

When God calls any of His servants to a great challenge—whether that servant is Joshua or Sergeant Ward or you or me—He always provides the encouragement we need to step up. And as God's words in these next few verses show, Joshua apparently needed *a lot* of encouragement (notice especially the phrases I have emphasized):

> *Be strong and courageous*, because you will lead these people to inherit the land I swore to their forefathers to give them. *Be strong and very courageous*. Be careful to obey all the law my servant Moses gave you; do not turn from it to the right or to the left, that you may be successful wherever you go. Do not let this Book of the Law depart from your mouth; meditate on it day and night, so that you may be careful to do everything written in it. Then you will be prosperous and successful. Have I not commanded you? *Be strong and courageous*. Do not be terrified; do not be discouraged, for the LORD your God will be with you wherever you go.
>
> (Josh. 1:6–9, emphasis added)

In these four verses, God encouraged Joshua—not one time, not two times, but *three times*. God saw that Joshua was perspiring and tugging at his collar, and that his knees were knocking, so He gave Joshua a triple dose of encouragement: "Be strong and courageous! . . . Be strong and very courageous! . . . Be strong and courageous!" Let's look at these encouragements more closely.

1. God Encouraged Joshua with His Promise

"Be strong and courageous," the Lord said, "because you will lead these people to inherit the land I swore to their forefathers to give them" (Josh. 1:6). God was referring to a promise He had made to Abraham six centuries earlier, and He had not forgotten His promise.

When you accept God's call, when you serve His purpose, when you share His message with others, you can do so courageously and confidently because God has promised that He will not fail you. You do not have to worry about being rejected by others. You do not have to be anxious about the results of your witness. You do not have to wonder what people will think of you. You do not have to concern yourself with opposition from your enemies or insults from your critics.

Why? Because you trust in the promises of God. When you know God always keeps His promises, you have confidence to step up in obedience to His call.

2. God Encouraged Joshua with the Power of His Word

"Be careful to obey all the law my servant Moses gave you," God said (Josh. 1:7)—and He went on to say that His Word was powerful. If you obey it, you experience its power firsthand. If you dwell in it and apply it to your daily life, you will be prosperous and successful.

God is not promising that everything will be easy. Joshua faced setbacks, opposition, and crises—and so will we. But if we obey God's Word and hold our ground, we will stand firm even though others around us may crumble. True prosperity and success come from holding tenaciously to the Word of God.

3. God Encouraged Joshua by His Presence

"Do not be terrified; do not be discouraged," He said, "for the LORD your God will be with you wherever you go" (Josh. 1:9). It appears that, after receiving those first two words of encouragement, Joshua was still shaking at the knees. God has reminded Joshua of His promise and His Word. But Joshua's confidence is still not quite strong enough.

So God gave Joshua a third word of encouragement. He told Joshua He would walk alongside him throughout his mission, throughout his battles, and throughout his crises. God knew what Joshua was thinking: *What good are promises and Scripture verses against giant-sized warriors armed with swords and spears?* So God saved the most powerful word of encouragement for last, telling Joshua in effect, "You will not face your battles alone. I will stick closer to you than your own skin."

On hearing that, Joshua was convinced. His courage was amply fortified. He said, in effect, "Yes, Lord! I'll step up."

What is the secret to victory in Joshua's life? The secret is that *there is no secret*! God has revealed everything to Joshua—and to us. When we live according to His promises and His Word, and when we trust in His presence moment by moment, He will give us the victory—guaranteed.

Behind the Eight Ball with Joshua

As you are probably aware, I am the pastor of a congregation in Atlanta called The Church of The Apostles. Our church is an evangelical, Anglican congregation committed to declaring the whole counsel of God. We believe that nothing we do is as important as obeying the words of Jesus in Matthew 24:14: "This gospel of the kingdom will be preached in the whole world as a testimony to all nations."

People sometimes ask me, "Why do you call your church 'The Church of The Apostles'? Is it because you believe in the teaching of the early apostles? Or is it because you believe that the people in your church have been sent out, as in the days of the apostles, as witnesses for Christ?"

My reply: for both reasons. We believe in the foundational teachings of the apostles—and we also believe we all are apostles, "sent ones," called to be the Lord's witnesses in our own communities and around the world. These are the reasons we use to explain the name of our church.

But there is another, very different reason that we are called "The Church of The Apostles." Two decades ago, when this church was founded, a man in authority in our denomination told me that this would be the name of our church. We would have no say in the matter.

You see, there is diversity of belief within the Anglican denomination, and there are people within the denomination who do not believe in preaching the gospel of the kingdom as a testimony to the whole world, in accordance with the command of the Lord. The man who gave our church its name was such an individual. Stated plainly, he did not approve of the evangelical stance of our congregation.

He looked me in the eye and said, "We don't need evangelicals and gospel-preaching churches in our denomination. Though we have agreed to allow you to start this church in Atlanta, there are two things I must tell you: First, don't leave your day job, because this church will fail in less than six months. Second, you are to name your congregation 'The Church of The Apostles.' Since you are determined to start a congregation of people who want to spread an evangelical gospel, this is how you will be known."

In other words, the name The Church of The Apostles was intended as a label of derision. We were being mocked as a church filled with little evangelical apostles who practiced an old-fashioned faith and went about preaching an outmoded, obsolete gospel.

Hearing that, I remembered that when the Lord's followers were first called "Christians" (meaning "Little Messiahs") at Antioch in Acts 11:26, it was a label of mockery and derision. And in the eighteenth century, when John Wesley ignited a revival movement accompanied by vigorous evangelistic and missionary activity, those believers were mocked and ridiculed. Their critics called them a bunch of "Methodists" because they methodically practiced such customs as receiving Communion, fasting, and abstaining from sin.

So I concluded that if our congregation was going to be labeled as an act of mockery over our desire to preach Christ, then we were in good company with great saints of the past. Knowing God can use even our critics for our good, I said to this man, "I am under authority. I will accept your direction. We will be called 'The Church of The Apostles.'"

That man passed away a number of years ago, but now, more than twenty years later, The Church of The Apostles—

which was supposed to fail within six months—is looking forward to the next twenty years. Over the years, we've had our ups and downs, but through it all, I always knew—and the congregation always knew—that this church was not Michael Youssef's idea. It was not the idea of any human authority or leader. It was not the figment of any human imagination. It was the result of a decision by God. When He said, "Step up," I obeyed and we trusted in His promises.

In the more than two decades of our existence as a church, our mission hasn't changed: we still preach the gospel of the kingdom in the whole world as a testimony to all nations. Our vision hasn't changed; it has only been brought into sharper focus. We are still a church of apostles, a congregation of "sent ones," believers sent by the Lord Jesus into the offices, shops, schools, neighborhoods, clubs, mission fields, and battlefields of our world.

Like Joshua, we have been called by God to step up, to be strong and courageous, and to accept the challenge, even though our knees are knocking. The Lord has promised us that we will accomplish our mission. If we trust in the Word of the Lord and meditate on it day and night, we will be successful. God Himself has promised us His presence and power—if we will *step up*.

My friend, I believe God is now calling *you* to step up and accept a new challenge for your life. That is why you are reading this book.

What was the chain of circumstances that placed this book in your hands? Did someone give it to you? Did you hear about it on the radio or TV? Did you just discover it by chance while browsing in the bookstore? However this book may have come into your possession, I don't believe it was an accident. God is challenging you to attempt something great in His name. He is calling you to step up and move out into a realm that He has promised you.

Perhaps there is a crisis, an opportunity, or a challenge in your life at this very moment. As you face this situation, you feel inadequate for the task. You lack confidence. You may even feel afraid. You are looking to heaven and asking God, *You want me to do* what? *You want me to step up and attempt the impossible?*

You are standing right behind the eight ball—and my friend, that's exactly where God wants you. You are standing in the very spot where Joshua himself once stood. You're asking God the same question that Joshua must have asked. And, like Joshua, you are standing on the threshold of a great work for God.

And the first thing God wants you to do is *step up!*

Prophets and Priests

In the Old Testament, God performed His work through prophets and priests. But in the New Testament, *all believers in Jesus Christ* are called to be prophets and priests.

What is a prophet? Most people think of a prophet as a person who *foretells* the future; but in the Bible, a prophet is a person who *tells forth* the will of God. A prophet calls people to repentance, obedience, renewal, and transformation. In Numbers 11:29, Moses said, "I wish that all the LORD's people were prophets and that the LORD would put his Spirit on them!"

These words were fulfilled when Peter, quoting God's words from the Old Testament, said, "In the last days . . . I will pour out my Spirit on all people. Your sons and daughters will prophesy, your young men will see visions, your old men will dream dreams" (Acts 2:17). Peter said this while speaking prophetically to a great crowd in Jerusalem. And when he called upon the people to repent and be baptized, *three thousand* responded and became followers of Jesus Christ (see Acts 2:14–41).

Though the Holy Spirit has given some Christians a *special* gift of prophecy, God expects *all* of His people to speak out prophetically, to call others to repentance, and to share with them the good news of Jesus Christ. In a very real sense, all believers are called to be prophets.

And we are also called to be priests. Peter wrote, "You are a chosen people, a royal priesthood, a holy nation, a people belonging to God, that you may declare the praises of him who called you out of darkness into his wonderful light" (1 Pet. 2:9). As a priest, you are called by God to minister to the people around you and to declare to them the glory and grace of God.

God has given you a unique mission to carry out as His prophet and priest. He has called you to undertake a task that *only you* can accomplish. No one else can do it for you. If you don't do it, it won't get done.

You cannot say to God, "That's not for me!" If God has called you to do it, then He will equip you and give you the confidence and courage to do it. When God calls us to do His work, He always gives us the encouragement we need, just as He encouraged Joshua three times. When He sets a challenge before you, all you have to supply is an obedient and willing heart. God supplies the rest.

What is the impossible task that God has called you to do? What does God want you to step up and accomplish as His chosen prophet and priest? Whatever that challenge may be, you now stand where Joshua stood. His task is now your task. His leadership challenge is now your leadership challenge. His calling is now your calling. And the encouragement and strength that God gave Joshua are now yours as well.

Looking Impossibility in the Face

In Joshua 6, we will come to the story of Joshua and the city of Jericho. You are undoubtedly familiar with the story—so familiar that you may have forgotten what a powerful story this is. In the account, God not only gives Joshua an impossible assignment—conquer the most heavily fortified city in Canaan—but He also saddles Joshua with a hopeless strategy: the army of Israel is to march around the city once a day for six days, then seven times in one day, then blow trumpets and shout. Does that sound like a winning military strategy—or does it sound like sheer madness?

Imagine Joshua standing before the walls of Jericho. What doubts must have gone though his mind! "Lord, this is an impossibility! The walls of that fortress are impenetrable! Do You know what You are asking? You want me to do *what*? March round and round, blow trumpets, and shout?"

Yet, as we shall see, Joshua was obedient to God's call upon his life. He accepted the impossible mission God had given him, and he accomplished it.

Perhaps the challenge God has set before you seems every bit as impossible as attacking a walled city with trumpets and shouts. The impossible mission God has given you might be to conquer your neighborhood, your workplace, or your campus with the good news of Jesus Christ.

Or the seemingly impossible mission God calls you to

might be a loving, gracious conquest of one specific person—a relative, a neighbor, a colleague, a fellow student. That person might seem totally resistant to God's Word and uninterested in a relationship with Jesus Christ. Just as Joshua once faced the fortified city walls of Jericho, you may be facing a stone wall of rejection.

God may even be calling you to be a witness to your worst enemy. He may be challenging you to reach out to someone who has hurt you, crushed you, and mistreated you. Sometimes the person with a harsh and hardened exterior is inwardly desperate, fearful, and needy. That person might seem completely self-sufficient on the outside while inwardly on the verge of total collapse. That individual is your Jericho. God has called you to reach out to that person and, by the power of His Spirit, bring down those walls.

Jerichos of the Twenty-first Century

This age of space exploration, computer technology, nuclear technology, and high-speed communication may seem totally removed from the age in which Joshua lived. Yet, at its core, life in Joshua's time was little different from life today. Joshua lived in a time of social crisis, political upheaval, moral indifference, spiritual confusion, and deadly opposition—just as we do today.

Everywhere you turn, you see Jerichos—walled fortresses of opposition, indifference, and resistance. Our society is encircled by terrorists who are committed to the destruction of the Western economic and social system, including the Christian faith. These terrorists have convinced themselves their cause is right. Many of them love death more than we love life. There is no way to reason with them or placate them or compromise with them, because they are 100 percent committed to our destruction. They patiently plot against us, certain that in time they will bring us to our knees. So these terrorists are a Jericho to us, because they threaten us externally.

But we also face an internal threat, a Jericho within. In our society, and even within the church, we see that more and more people love ease and material comfort. They have opted for the good life, the soft life. They say they believe in God and in Jesus, but their "faith" is mere easy believe-ism, not biblical Christianity. In other words, they mentally agree with Christian doctrines, but they act like people of the world. They live to please themselves, not Christ; they pursue worldly goals, not the goals of His kingdom; they seek earthly wealth and security, not the bold and risky adventure of faith.

This kind of "soft-core Christianity" has been around for a long time. As Protestant theologian H. Richard Niebuhr wrote in *The Kingdom of God in America* (1937), many Christians seem to believe that a "God without wrath brought men without sin into a kingdom without judgment through the ministrations of a Christ without a cross."[2] Indeed, Jesus Himself said to the rich, self-satisfied church in Laodicea, "Because you are lukewarm—neither hot nor cold—I am about to spit you out of my mouth" (Rev. 3:16).

Increasingly, people around us are turning away from a belief in objective proof. They have abandoned intellectual rigor and rational thinking in favor of shallow emotions. They prefer to do what *feels* right rather than do what *is* right. Commentator George G. Hunter III describes our current culture this way:

The Church, in the Western world, faces populations who are increasingly "secular"—people with no Christian memory, who don't know what we Christians are talking about. These populations are increasingly "urban"—and out of touch with God's "natural revelation." These populations are increasingly "postmodern"; they have graduated from Enlightenment ideology and are more peer-driven, feeling-driven, and "right-brain" than their forebears. These populations are increasingly "neo-barbarian"; they lack "refinement" or "class," and their lives are often out of control. These populations are increasingly receptive—exploring worldview options from Astrology to Zen—and are often looking "in all the wrong places" to make sense of their lives and find their soul's true home.[3]

In the midst of such a culture, people are crying out for a few Christian believers who are committed, who are courageous, who are willing to step up and speak out as prophets and priests to our generation. Our world is crying out for a few believers who love God and His Word more than their own comfort.

And, I believe, God is calling *you* to step up and become one of those courageous, committed believers. He has chosen *you* as one of His prophets, as one of His royal priests.

Content to Live in the Shadows

The book of Joshua opens with these words: "After the death of Moses. . . ." So Moses is dead and God calls upon Joshua to step up. Here again, we see a parallel between the day of Joshua and our own day.

In the past, we in the church have largely relied upon the

clergy—ministers and evangelists and missionaries, people we think of as "professional Christians"—to do the work of spreading the good news of Jesus Christ in our society and around our world. But the day of the "professional Christian" is over. We live in a postmodern, post-Christian world. The day in which people would listen to evangelists and preachers has passed.

Dan Kimball is pastor of Vintage Faith in Santa Cruz, California, home to UC Santa Cruz, which he described as "one of the more anti-Christian campuses in California." He decided to go to the campus to interview students and find out what they thought about Jesus and the church.

He discovered that many of the students admired Jesus, viewing Him as a wise teacher, a liberator, and an enlightened "guru." But those same students didn't like the church. They felt that the church had turned the teachings of Jesus into legalistic rules while corrupting His message of love. Kimball reflected that the students "definitely liked Jesus, but they did not like the Church."

Kimball decided to get out of his office and learn more about how the world viewed the church. He started taking his books and laptop to a local coffeehouse to do his sermon study. There he developed friendships with the coffeehouse customers and baristas. He listened instead of talking, and he began to discover why today's "post-Christian twenty- and thirty-somethings" didn't like pastors and didn't trust the church. He found, for example, that they viewed the church as too political, too negative and judgmental, too male-dominated, and too arrogant.[4]

Bottom line: Today's younger generation does not want to come into the church and listen to preachers preach. But they do like Jesus. Their image of Jesus may be skewed, but they do respect Him. They are open to talking about spirituality and faith in a relaxed setting, such as a coffeehouse or the campus commons.

If we want to reach today's generation with the gospel of Jesus Christ, we have to go where the people are. We need to make friends with non-Christians. There are people all around us who are willing to talk about Jesus and hear about His love. They will never be reached by a pastor or an evangelist. The only person who can reach them is *you*.

The death of Moses made it necessary for Joshua to step up and stand in that gap. In the same way, the end of the era of evangelists and preachers is a symbolic "death of Moses." Now God calls us, as a generation of a twenty-first-century Joshuas, to step up and stand in the gap.

Who is going to make a difference for God in today's world? Answer: you, the person reading this book.

You, the homemaker. You, the businessman. You, the student. You, the health-care worker or public safety worker or soldier or lawyer or engineer or journalist or educator or factory worker or retiree. Whatever your walk in life, wherever you find yourself, you are a twenty-first-century Joshua. You are the one God has commissioned for this task at this moment in history.

I know you have misgivings. I know you feel inadequate. You're thinking, *God wants me to step up and do* what? *He wants me to be a witness* where? *He wants me to reach out to* whom? *I'm not a leader. I'm not a preacher. I am certainly no Joshua. If I try to share the message of Christ with someone else, I'll just make a mess of things. I just want to be an everyday, ordinary Christian. I just want to mind my own business and go to church on Sundays and have my needs met.*

If that's how you feel, you're not alone. When Joshua heard what God wanted him to do, his heart probably jumped up into his throat and stuck there. That's why God had to encourage him three times. I think Joshua was very content to live in the shadow of Moses. When God said, "Step up," Joshua wanted to take a step back. But God's work would not be accomplished until Joshua stepped up and filled the gap left by Moses.

And the same is true in your life and mine: the work of the Lord in our generation will not be accomplished until you and I and all the other Joshuas of our day step up and become true prophets and priests of our Lord. We must begin by stepping up.

It's normal to feel inadequate. In fact, God *wants* you to feel inadequate in your own strength so you will rely on Him for all your needs. "Seek first his kingdom and his righteousness," Jesus said, "and all these things will be given to you as well" (Matt. 6:33). In other words, when we accept God's call upon our lives and pursue His kingdom and His righteousness with a whole heart, He will supply all our needs according to His riches in Christ Jesus.

Perhaps you became aware of God's call on your life only as you have been reading these words. But God didn't call you to be His Joshua in the last half hour or yesterday or sometime last week. Just as God spent forty years preparing Joshua for the conquest of the promised land, God has been preparing you for your great challenge. He called you by name before you were born. Throughout your life, He has been bringing people, experiences, and insights into your life to shape and equip you for this very moment. He is encouraging you right now. He will continue to minister to you through His Word, His Spirit, and His people.

God's Side of the Equation

Mercury Morris and Art Fowler make an unlikely team. First, let me tell you about Mercury Morris.

Every football fan in the 1970s knew the exploits of Miami Dolphins star running back Mercury Morris. He helped lead the Dolphins to three consecutive Super Bowls, including back-to-back victories in Super Bowls VII and VIII. He ran for exactly one thousand yards during the Dolphins history-making undefeated season in 1972.

Though Mercury Morris was nimble and sure-footed on the football field, he stumbled badly after his retirement from the game. In 1982, he was convicted of cocaine trafficking and sentenced to twenty years in prison. That's where Art Fowler comes in.

Art is an ordinary Christian with an extraordinary desire to reach people for Christ. He lives in Castle Rock, Colorado. In a coffee shop or supermarket checkout line, he will often strike up a conversation with someone he's never met before. As they talk, Art shares with that person the good news of Jesus Christ. Hundreds of people have come to know Christ through Art Fowler's informal, one-on-one ministry.

In 1982, he opened his newspaper and read the story of Mercury Morris's conviction on drug-trafficking charges. Though Art had never met or spoken with Mercury Morris, he knew the fallen football star needed to hear about Jesus Christ. So he bought a plane ticket and flew to Miami. Once there, he talked his way into the Florida prison where Morris was held, and the former football star agreed to meet with him.

Art sat down with Mercury in a visitation room at the prison and told him that, in spite of his imprisonment, God wanted to save him and use him. "Mercury was open," Art recalls. "He was ready. And he prayed to receive Christ on the spot. Then he said to me, 'Art, I want you to go see my wife, Bobbie, and tell her what you just told me. I want my whole family to know about Jesus.'"

Art went to Mercury's house and knocked on the door. Bobbie Morris answered the door, and Art explained that he had just come from visiting her husband in prison. "She was there with her kids," Art recalls, "and we talked, and she accepted Jesus as Lord of her life too."

In 1986, Mercury Morris's conviction was overturned by the Florida Supreme Court and he was granted a new trial. He reached a plea deal with the prosecutors that sentenced him to three years—the time he had already served. Mercury Morris was a free man—both legally free and free in Christ. Today, Mercury Morris is a Christian motivational speaker.

In an interview that aired several years ago on Dr. D. James Kennedy's syndicated television broadcast, Mercury Morris recalled his life-changing encounter with Art Fowler. "I have a lot of trophies," he said. "They're all over the house. But the only trophies I have out on display are the ones that are the most significant to me. One of the things of significance I keep out is a plaque with a little football player on it that I got from Art Fowler back in 1987. It reads, 'I can do all things through Christ who strengthens me.'"

So Mercury Morris and Art Fowler are teammates, playing on the same winning team with Jesus Christ and Joshua—and with you and me. "Art Fowler is my teammate in the spiritual sense," Mercury says today. "Coach Don Shula and the Miami Dolphins, that's one thing. But Art Fowler and Jesus Christ, that's another."[5]

Let's put ourselves in Art Fowler's place. Suppose you and I had opened the newspaper and we saw the story about Mercury Morris's drug conviction. Suppose we felt God tugging at our hearts, challenging us to step up. How would we have responded?

I can tell you right now, I would have thought, *You want me to do* what? *You want me to fly halfway across the country? You want me to talk my way into a prison and share Christ with a man who doesn't know me from Adam?* But Art Fowler answered that call.

What would happen if every person reading these words became like Art Fowler? Imagine if there were thousands of Art Fowlers around this country, sharing the gospel with strangers in coffee shops and checkout lines and prisons, wherever and whenever God opened a door and issued a call. How many lives would be changed as a result?

You may be thinking, *I want to be like that—but I can't do that. I haven't even told any of my neighbors or coworkers I am a Christian. I have never witnessed about Christ to a single soul! The very thought of talking to someone about Jesus Christ makes my knees wobble!* Like Joshua, you are looking at that fortified city and you see a stone wall of impossibility.

What went through Joshua's mind when God told him to take that city in His name? I imagine he thought about the fact that the Israelites were a young nation of ex-slaves who had spent forty years wandering in the desert. Militarily, the

Israelites were a ragtag army of wandering tent-dwellers, ill-equipped for battle. They faced an ancient civilization with a long tradition of military might—and their enemies were secure behind fortified walls of stone.

But there was one more factor on the Israelites' side of the equation: God Himself. When the Lord issued His challenge, He told Joshua, "Do not be terrified; do not be discouraged, for the Lord your God will be with you wherever you go." When Joshua weighed all the factors on both sides of the equation, he knew everything he needed to know. And that is why Joshua, despite the impossibility of the task, and despite his own sense of inadequacy, chose to accept that mission.

Joshua stepped up because he had full confidence in his Lord. No matter how impossible the task God has called us to, we can step up in that same confidence.

Carried by the Lord

Henry Moorhouse was a nineteenth-century English preacher who had a great influence on the American evangelist Dwight L. Moody. Moorhouse had a daughter, Minnie, who was paralyzed from the waist down, and her affliction weighed heavily on his soul. He was also feeling weighed down by struggles and opposition in other areas of his life and his ministry.

One day, Moorhouse came home with a package for his wife. As he entered the front door, he saw his daughter sitting in a chair. He bent down and kissed her, then he said, "Where is Mother? I have a package for her."

"Mommy is upstairs," the little girl said. "Can I give her the package, Daddy?"

"Well, Minnie," Moorhouse said, "how can you carry a package? You can't even carry yourself upstairs."

The girl smiled. "Oh, Daddy, that's easy! I'll carry the package while you carry me!"

At that moment, Henry Moorhouse experienced a flash of spiritual insight. He realized that even though he was carrying burdens in his life that seemed too heavy to bear, he himself was being carried by the Lord Jesus Christ.[6]

And that's exactly what God will do for you and me when we step up and answer His call. No matter how impossible the challenge may seem, God will carry us. That was His promise to Joshua, and that is His promise to us today.

God promised the land of Canaan to Israel. That is why Canaan was called "the promised land." God promised to carry Israel across the Jordan River. He promised to carry Israel past the walls of Jericho. He promised to carry Israel into a land that flowed with milk and honey.

But Israel had to step up. The Israelites had to trust in God, obey His instructions, and do His will. And so it is with you and me.

God never assigns a task or issues a challenge without making a provision. God never gives a command without a promise. God has called you, and He will not abandon you, forsake you, or leave you in the lurch. We can step up in confidence and courage, knowing that even though our knees are knocking and our hands are trembling, He is always with us.

2

You Want Me to Go into Enemy Territory?

Joshua 2

The most successful and celebrated spy in the history of modern Israel was a man named Eli Cohen. Born in Egypt in 1924, he began working with Israeli military intelligence in 1960. Assuming the guise of a Syrian Arab named Kamel Amin Tsa'abet, Cohen established a false identity in Argentina, then moved to Damascus, Syria—deep within the territory of one of Israel's most bitter enemies.

There, Eli Cohen reportedly befriended many officials of the Syrian government, including Amin Hafiz, who eventually became prime minister. Cohen was so convincing that Hafiz actually considered appointing the Israeli spy to the position of deputy defense minister!

Cohen studied the Syrian fortifications on the Golan Heights, then made recommendations to the government that eucalyptus trees be planted around bunkers and artillery emplacements that targeted Israel. Cohen told the Syrians that the trees would provide camouflage and shade. After the Syrian military took his suggestion and planted the trees, Cohen informed Israel's military intelligence.

In January 1965, Soviet counterespionage agents tracked coded radio signals to Eli Cohen—and they arrested him. Though Cohen was hanged in Syria on May 18, 1965, the information he provided before his death gave Israel the victory in the Six-Day War two years later. The Israeli air force simply targeted the stands of newly planted eucalyptus trees—and they were able to easily destroy most of the Syrian military installations on the Golan Heights. For his role in that victory, Eli Cohen is remembered as a hero in Israel to this day.[1]

The story of Eli Cohen has many parallels to the ancient spy story we find in Joshua 2. The biblical account describes an espionage mission that took place three thousand years ago. In that account, Joshua sent two Israelite spies on a risky mission deep into enemy territory—and their courageous exploits resulted in victory for the Israelites!

An Old Testament Spy Thriller

As this tale of ancient espionage opens, we read: "Joshua son of Nun secretly sent two spies from Shittim. 'Go, look over the land,' he said, 'especially Jericho.' So they went and entered the house of a prostitute named Rahab and stayed there" (Josh. 2:1).

The two Israelite spies went behind enemy lines and penetrated enemy territory, and God directed them to the house of a dishonorable and despised woman: a Canaanite prostitute named Rahab. The two spies saw her not as a prostitute, but as a woman who desperately needed to be saved. So the spies made a bargain with her. "Our lives for your lives!" the spies told her. "If you don't tell what we are doing, we will treat you and your family kindly and faithfully when the Lord gives us the land."

These two spies never lost sight of their mission. They came to Jericho for a specific purpose. They entered enemy territory to win victory for God's cause—and to rescue Rahab and her family when they turned to the Lord for help.

As I read this story, I can't help thinking of another Old Testament character, a man who went into enemy territory—but instead of going there to serve God and save people from the coming destruction, he went into the land of the enemy and became one of them. His name was Lot, and the enemy city where he lived was called Sodom. In Genesis 19 we see that, instead of living as a shining light for God in that dark city, Lot blended into the shadows of moral compromise. Instead of standing strong for God, he bargained away his integrity.

Unlike Lot, the two spies who entered Jericho understood they were on a mission. God gave them a challenge, and they accepted that challenge as an opportunity to minister to the desperate needs of Rahab and her family. They refused to compromise with sin and evil because they had come to defeat it.

Somehow, word reached the king of Jericho that spies had entered the home of this prostitute. So the king sent a message to Rahab: "Bring out the men who came to you and entered your house, because they have come to spy out the whole land" (Josh. 2:3). Instead of obeying the order of the king, Rahab hid the two spies under stalks of flax on her rooftop. Then she sent word back to the king that the spies had departed. "Go after them quickly," she said. "You may catch up with them" (2:5).

That night, Rahab went to the roof and helped the two

Israelite spies escape from the city. Because her house was built into the city wall, she was able to let the two spies down by a rope from her window. Before the two spies melted into the darkness, they told Rahab that when the army of Israel returned to destroy the city, she should display a scarlet cord in the window. The Israelite soldiers would see that bloodred cord and spare her house and everyone inside.

So the spies returned to Joshua and told him, "The LORD has surely given the whole land into our hands; all the people are melting in fear because of us" (Josh. 2:24).

How should we apply this ancient story to our lives today? Is this merely an Old Testament spy thriller? Or does the adventure of these two Israelite spies still have something to say to us across all these centuries? Stay tuned!

We Are Aliens

The story of Joshua 2 is the story of two faithful, committed believers on a mission. And just like these two Old Testament spies, you and I are on a mission, sent by God behind enemy lines. And since you are on a *mission*, what else would you be but a *missionary*? Perhaps you never thought of yourself as a missionary before, but that's exactly what you are as a follower of Christ. And wherever you live and work and spend your time is your "mission field."

So you must ask yourself: *Am I carrying out the mission God has given me? As I live and work in enemy territory, am I maintaining my focus on my mission, like those two Israelite spies in Jericho? Or have I blended in with my environment like Lot? Am I achieving my mission—or have I compromised my mission? Have I lost sight of the reason God sent me into enemy territory in the first place?*

Imagine if the two Israelite spies had gone into Canaan and said to each other, "These people are wealthy and powerful. They enjoy a lifestyle of luxury. Are we sure we ought to go to war against this city? I wouldn't mind having some of these luxuries for myself! Maybe we can make a deal with these people. Maybe we can blend in, stay a while, and enjoy the good things this city has to offer." Imagine if, instead of staying focused on their mission, these two spies had decided to compromise their mission.

But they didn't. They remembered that they had entered enemy territory in order to fulfill God's plan for their lives, and for His kingdom. And that is a profound lesson for your life and mine.

We dare not forget that this world is not our true home. We are aliens, temporarily sent into enemy territory. Our citizenship is in heaven, not here, behind enemy lines. When we are in the neighborhood, the workplace, the marketplace, or on the campus, we are on a mission. We are fulfilling God's strategy.

So instead of compromising with the enemy culture that surrounds us, with all of its enticements, pleasures, and luxuries that would divert us from our goal, we need to stay focused on our mission. We need always to remember the real reason God sent us into enemy territory.

It's a mistake to assume that God sent the spies into Jericho only to gather intelligence. God also sent the spies into Jericho to rescue Rahab and her family. He had a plan for Rahab's life.

In Matthew 1:5, we see that Rahab, the Canaanite prostitute, is included in the genealogy of Jesus of Nazareth. The two spies didn't know it, but by rescuing Rahab and her family, they were helping to fulfill Old Testament prophecy by preserving the lineage of the coming Messiah. We never know what God may choose to bring forth when we respond to Him in obedience.

Who Is Your "Rahab"?

God has sent us into enemy territory to rescue the "Rahabs" in our midst. He has sent us to reach out to the despised and disreputable ones, to the least and the last and the lost. He has sent us to share the good news of Jesus Christ with prostitutes, prisoners, addicts, and alcoholics, and all of the other down-and-outers. He has also sent us to share the good news with the rich, the powerful, and the "up-and-outers," because their lives are miserable and empty too.

We may not feel drawn to such people. We may not want to be around them. The two Jewish spies in Jericho probably didn't have a very high opinion of Rahab, the Gentile prostitute. But we have been sent to such people nonetheless. We have been sent to share God's love with them and to accept them just as they are.

We Christians often make the mistake of thinking that people need to clean up their lives before they can be saved. That's simply not true, as the Scriptures make clear. If people had to clean themselves up before coming to God, it would negate the grace of God. As Charlotte Elliott wrote in the hymn "Just As I Am,"

> *Just as I am, and waiting not*
> *To rid my soul of one dark blot,*
> *To Thee, whose blood can cleanse each spot,*
> *O Lamb of God, I come! I come!*

Human beings do not have the power to rid their souls of even one blot of sin. It is God's job to cleanse. Those who are stained and defiled by sin need only to accept and receive God's cleansing. They need only to come "just as" they are.

We do a great disservice to people by making them feel they must look like us, act like us, dress like us, and live like us before they can be saved. God help us, that is not the message of the gospel. The good news of Jesus Christ is that God has reached down to sinners right where they are. God saves—from the gutter-most to the uttermost. God redeems those the world says are beyond redemption. God never gives up on any of His own, not even those who have given up on themselves.

Jesus saved the prostitutes, the tax collectors, the adulterers, the ones the Pharisees thought were beyond the reach of God's love. The very fact that God chose to save a Gentile prostitute along with her household serves as an encouragement to us all. No matter what you or I have done, God's grace is still available. No matter what your crime, no matter how rebellious you may have been, no matter how deep your shame and regret, God will save you, redeem your life, and use you in a mighty way if you repent and turn to Him.

And God makes the same offer to everyone around you—including people who have hurt you, people you simply can't stand. God wants to save and redeem your foulmouthed boss, your immoral coworker, your addicted fellow student, your bitter atheist professor, your angry, obnoxious neighbor. No one is beyond the reach of God's grace—and He has strategically placed you in enemy territory so you can be a witness and a blessing to the Rahabs who are all around you.

Of course, if we are to reach out and rescue the Rahabs

in our midst, we must be distinct from them. If we share the gospel with our coworkers, we must give them a reason to want our gospel. If our own lifestyles, our ethics, our speech, and our behavior are no better than theirs, what do we have to offer them? What are we rescuing them from if our way of life is no different from theirs? If we are not distinct from the world around us, if we simply blend in, we have compromised with the enemy—and all our witnessing will fall on deaf ears.

So who is your "Rahab"? And how will you reach that person for Christ?

An Astonishing Statement of Faith

As you think about this story, you may wonder: *Was it right for Rahab to lie in order to protect the spies?* The answer: *No!* It is never right to do wrong, even with good intentions. The Bible reports Rahab's actions, but it does not approve them. At this point in her life, Rahab had heard about the God of Israel—but she had not yet experienced Him.

This is important to remember in our own lives as we work and witness behind enemy lines. As you carry out your mission in your workplace, your neighborhood, or your school, you will be amazed at the people who respond to your witness. Some who seem indifferent or even openly hostile to Christ will do an about-face. Some who seem opposed to you may actually be watching you, listening to you, observing how you respond under pressure, and testing the authenticity of your Christian character and witness.

Imagine the astonishment of the two spies when they heard this Gentile prostitute declare her faith in God:

I know that the LORD has given this land to you and that a great fear of you has fallen on us, so that all who live in this country are melting in fear because of you. We have heard how the LORD dried up the water of the Red Sea for you when you came out of Egypt, and what you did to Sihon and Og, the two kings of the Amorites east of the Jordan, whom you completely destroyed. When we heard of it, our hearts melted and everyone's courage failed because of you, for the LORD your God is God in heaven above and on the earth below.

(Josh. 2:9–11)

While it is important to be equipped for the task of witnessing, and while we should have as much understanding of the Scriptures as we can, we don't need a PhD in apologetics to share Christ with the people around us. All we need is to trust that God is going ahead of us, preparing the hearts of those who need Him. That is why we pray God will prepare their hearts, just as He prepared the heart of Rahab.

When Rahab shared her budding faith with these two spies, she gave them all the encouragement they needed to carry on with their mission. She told them God had already terrified the powerful Canaanite king in Jericho. She told them all they needed to do was to walk in and take the promised land away from the godless inhabitants.

Why were the Canaanites so terrified of the Israelites—of this ragtag band of wandering former slaves? In truth, it was not the Israelites themselves who terrified the Canaanites. As Rahab's words show, the true object of the Canaanites' fear was the God of the Israelites and His almighty power. But while all the other Canaanite people were melting in fear before the God of Israel, one woman, Rahab the prostitute, made a choice to turn to the Israelites' God for refuge.

I believe there are people within your sphere of influence who are at the same place Rahab was. God has prepared their hearts. He is drawing them to Himself. And now He has placed you in a strategic position to reach them with the gospel. They have been living in fear, in anguish, in sorrow, in loneliness. They are saying to themselves, *I've heard that Jesus saves and heals and transforms lives. I've heard that Jesus gives strength to the weak and liberates the addicted. I've heard that He sets the prisoner free and binds the brokenhearted.*

And they are waiting for you to tell them about Him. They want to hear you tell your story about how Jesus set you free from all the hurts and hindrances that bound you. They want to hear you say, "Let me tell you my story. Let me tell you how Jesus set me free from failure, shame, worry, fear, and hopelessness. Let me tell you how He forgave all my sins and took away all my guilt and gave me a new robe of righteousness that can never be taken away."

And when you tell your story to the Rahabs in your life, they will say to you, "Where have you been all my life?" And you will probably have to say with some regret, "I have been here all the time. But I kept my mouth shut. I'm sorry."

Don't keep your mouth shut one day longer. Rescue the Rahab in your life. Point the way to the Source of mercy and forgiveness you have found. The same overflowing grace that changed the heart of a Canaanite prostitute is available for all who receive it.

Know Your Enemy

Thirty centuries have come and gone since those two spies hid under sheaves of flax on a Jericho rooftop. In that time, the business of spying has grown much more sophisticated and complicated. Spies today employ a bewildering array of abbreviations to describe their intelligence-gathering activities. There's COMINT (short for COMmunications INTelligence), which involves eavesdropping on phone calls. There's ELINT (ELectronic INTelligence), which involves intercepting electronic signals. IMINT (IMagery INTelligence) is spying by taking photos from airplanes or space satellites.

But ask any intelligence expert what is the most effective form of spying, and he will probably say: HUMINT—HUMan INTelligence, the risky business of putting spies behind enemy lines. Intercepted messages and aerial photographs can yield important information. But if you really want to know what's going on inside enemy territory, you must have human spies on the ground, penetrating the government, observing military activities, and getting the enemy to reveal information. Whether wars are fought with cruise missiles and smart bombs or swords and spears, the key to victory has always involved placing human beings on the ground behind enemy lines.

This principle is equally true when it comes to spreading the good news of Jesus Christ. I don't say this because I'm antitechnology. I'm grateful for such technologies as radio, television, and the Internet, and I utilize all of these amazing electronic media as a minister and evangelist. Technology is a wonderful tool—but it can never be a complete substitute for human interaction.

God wants people who are willing to go into enemy territory, Satan's territory, and to reach people where they work and live. God wants people who are willing to plant their feet in enemy territory and claim it for Jesus Christ.

Our goal is to rescue lost human souls, to free them from the enemy's oppression, and to show them the way to the abundant life in Christ. To truly impact people who are on the other side of the spiritual divide, we must meet them face-to-face. We must build relationships on genuine caring, not merely on making as many converts as possible.

Everyone who is not a citizen of the kingdom of heaven is a captive in Satan's domain. God calls us, wherever we are, to go into enemy territory, to share the good news of Jesus Christ, and to rescue people from the control of Satan. C. S. Lewis put it this way in *Mere Christianity*: "Enemy-occupied territory, that is what the world is. Christianity is the story of how the rightful King has landed, you might say landed in disguise, and is calling us all to take part in a great campaign of sabotage."[2]

Whom do we seek to sabotage? Satan!

Don't think for a moment God is calling you to attack any human being. Your non-Christian coworkers, your nonbelieving fellow students, and your antagonistic neighbors are *not* your enemies. They may treat you as an enemy. They may be hostile to the gospel. They may even cheat you, bully you, lie about you, and make you miserable—but they are not the enemy.

In fact, the reason they behave in such hurtful and hateful ways is that they are living under the enemy's power. They are slaves to the enemy's dictates. That's why they exhibit characteristics of the enemy.

But we must never forget who our true enemy is. As the apostle Paul told us, "Our struggle is not against flesh and blood, but against the rulers, against the authorities, against the powers of this dark world and against the spiritual forces of evil in the heavenly realms" (Eph. 6:12). Our enemy is Satan. He is the one we fight.

Your career and your place in the world are God's gifts to you. He has strategically positioned you where you are because He has a plan for your life. That is your mission field. That is the place where God has called you to be His fisherman, casting your net for the souls of men and women and children.

Every human encounter in your life is a God-given opportunity for you to invade Satan's territory and win another battle for Christ. Every person you meet is someone who could become your brother or sister in Christ. Even a person who hates you or hurts you could one day become your dearest friend in Christ.

So when you're attacked, don't retaliate. Love with the love of Jesus Christ. Look beyond your hurt and annoyance, and see with the eyes of Christ. Pray for the unsaved and ask God to use you to help set them free—then watch and see how God answers your prayer.

From Enemy to Brother

In my previous book, *Fifteen Secrets to a Wonderful Life: Mastering the Art of Positive Living*, I told the story of an American flier in World War II, Jake DeShazer. I recently came across the story of a Japanese airman in World War II, and the amazing impact that Jake DeShazer had on the life of this

Japanese pilot. The pilot's name is Mitsuo Fuchida. Let me tell you his amazing story.

As a boy growing up in Japan, Mitsuo Fuchida dreamed of becoming a samurai, a noble warrior who would bring glory to the Land of the Rising Sun. Trained as a fighter pilot, Mitsuo graduated from the military academy at age twenty-one. As Imperial Japan was enlarging its empire, the leaders of Japan chose Mitsuo Fuchida to lead an aerial attack that would deal a fatal blow to the United States Pacific Fleet.

Early on the morning of Sunday, December 7, 1941, Mitsuo Fuchida climbed into his fighter plane and took off from the deck of a Japanese aircraft carrier. He led a force of nearly two hundred planes on a mission to attack the Americans at a place called Pearl Harbor.

At 7:49 a.m., he radioed the battle cry to his fellow pilots: "Tora! Tora! Tora!" In an attack that lasted less than two hours, Mitsuo and his fellow pilots destroyed two mighty American battleships, two destroyers, a minelayer, and 188 airplanes; they left ten other ships seriously damaged. The Japanese attack killed 2,333 Americans and left 1,139 wounded.

As they flew away from the scene of battle, Mitsuo and his fellow pilots celebrated a stunning victory over the Americans. Japanese losses were light—only twenty-nine airplanes lost and fewer than sixty airmen killed or wounded.

Thus began the war between the United States and Imperial Japan. That war lasted more than three and a half years. During that time, Mitsuo Fuchida fought many battles in the skies over the Pacific. He narrowly escaped death many times.

In June 1942, he was on the aircraft carrier *Akagi*, undergoing emergency surgery for appendicitis. His doctor told him to stay in the ship's infirmary to rest, but when he heard the sound of battle, he disobeyed the doctor and went up on the flight deck. The battle of Midway had just begun. American planes attacked his ship, dropping bombs that penetrated to the lower decks. Everyone in the ship's infirmary was killed in the attack. Though he broke both ankles while fighting fires during the battle, Mitsuo Fuchida survived the battle of Midway because he disobeyed his doctor's orders.

In the summer of 1945, Mitsuo Fuchida was attending a weeklong conference at a military base outside a major city on the island of Honshu. He received orders to leave that base and fly to Tokyo. He flew his fighter-bomber out of that city on August 5. Just hours after he departed, an American bomber dropped an atomic bomb on that Japanese city—a city called Hiroshima. The entire city and the military base were destroyed, and once again Mitsuo's life was spared.

The atomic bomb ended the war. Japan was defeated. Mitsuo Fuchida, who had dreamed of being a noble samurai warrior, was bitter and disillusioned. One day, months after the end of the war, Mitsuo was in a train station in Japan when an American missionary handed him a leaflet.

The leaflet, printed in Japanese, was called *I Was a Prisoner of Japan*. It was written by Jake DeShazer, an American airman who had flown on a surprise bombing raid over Tokyo in 1942. Mitsuo boarded the train and read the leaflet as the train pulled out of the station.

In the leaflet, DeShazer told the story of that bombing raid. As his bomber ran out of fuel, he bailed out over Japanese-held China. He was captured and spent the rest of the war in a Japanese POW camp. In the prison camp, he was often beaten and he suffered from dysentery. In the course of his ordeal, DeShazer became filled with bitterness and hatred for his Japanese captors.

After DeShazer had spent two years in captivity, the Japanese allowed the prisoners to have a Bible for three weeks. The prisoners tore the Bible into sections and passed it around. With only one tiny slit of sunlight to read by, Jake devoured the Scriptures, memorizing as much as he could. By the time the Bible was taken away from him, Jake had committed his life to Jesus Christ.

After his conversion, Jake sensed Jesus saying to him, "Love your enemies and pray for those who persecute you" (Matt. 5:44). So Jake began to talk to a guard who had often beaten him and mistreated him. Jake asked the guard about his family and his home, and the guard was amazed at Jake's kindness. In response, the guard began to show kindness to Jake by bringing him extra food.

While he was still in prison, Jake realized God had planted within him a love for the Japanese people. So, after the war ended and he was released from prison, Jake returned to Japan as a missionary. He shared the love of Christ with the very people on whom he had once dropped bombs. The land Jake DeShazer had once considered enemy territory became his home.

As Mitsuo Fuchida read Jake DeShazer's story, something stirred within him. He wanted to know more about this life-changing man named Jesus. He obtained a Bible and began reading, and he was struck by the words of Jesus in Luke 23:34: "Father, forgive them, for they do not know what they are doing." As a result, one day in 1950, Mitsuo Fuchida—the man who had led the attack on Pearl Harbor—accepted Jesus Christ as his Lord and Savior.

Mitsuo immediately began sharing his faith. The first time he spoke at an evangelistic rally, five hundred Japanese people committed their lives to Jesus Christ. Mitsuo Fuchida became a preacher and an evangelist, and people began calling him "the Billy Graham of Japan."

One day, Mitsuo decided to seek out the man who had written the leaflet that changed the course of his life. He looked up the address of Jake DeShazer and went to the home of the American missionary. When DeShazer answered the door, the former Japanese pilot said, "My name is Mitsuo Fuchida."

DeShazer instantly recognized him—and he smiled. "Come in!" As soon as Mitsuo Fuchida crossed the threshold, Jake DeShazer reached out and embraced him. The two former enemies were now brothers in Christ.[3]

God sent Joshua into the enemy territory of Jericho to save Rahab and her family from the coming destruction. And God sent Jake DeShazer back to the people who had once been his enemies to bring them the good news of salvation. Now God calls you and me, as Christians, to go into the enemy-held territory of this world—into our workplaces and neighborhoods and schools. Our mission is not to search and destroy but to seek and save. God calls us to reach out to those, like Rahab, who are lost in sin and enslaved by Satan—and to bring them safely into God's kingdom of love.

3

You Want Me to Cross the River of Impossibility?

Joshua 3–4

Born in Russia in 1874, Chaim Weizmann was a Jewish biochemist who invented a process for producing acetone through bacterial fermentation. Educated in Germany and Switzerland, he moved to England where he pursued his scientific research.

While in England, Weizmann emerged as a central figure in the Zionist movement. The Jewish people had been without a nation of their own ever since the Roman army under Titus sacked Jerusalem and destroyed the temple in AD 70. The goal of Weizmann and his fellow Zionists was to restore the Jewish people to their homeland.

During the 1920s, Weizmann forged friendly ties with Arab leaders, including King Faisal I of Iraq. He helped lay the groundwork for a functional Jewish society in Israel by working with Albert Einstein to establish Hebrew University in Jerusalem in 1921. The dream of reestablishing a Jewish nation after centuries of diaspora (the dispersal of the Jewish people all around the world) occupied all of Weizmann's adult life, from his attendance at Zionist conferences in the late 1800s until his death in 1952. For most of his life, the dream of a Jewish homeland seemed utterly impossible, yet he never abandoned hope.

In the early years of Weizmann's association with the Zionist movement in England, he formed an alliance with British political leader Arthur Balfour. It was a frustrating relationship for Weizmann. Although Balfour supported the idea of a Jewish homeland, he wanted that homeland to be located not in Palestine, but in Uganda, a beautiful but remote nation in east-central Africa.

Weizmann repeatedly tried to explain to Balfour that the Jewish people had historical and spiritual ties to Palestine, the land of Abraham, Isaac, and Jacob. But Balfour insisted that one piece of land was as good as another, and the Jews should be happy to have a homeland in Africa.

Finally, in a last-ditch effort to get his point across to Balfour, Weizmann said, "Just imagine, Mr. Balfour, that I could move all Londoners from London to Paris. After all, Paris is a beautiful city—and as you say, one piece of land is as good as another. Would you and your fellow Londoners accept such an offer?"

Balfour frowned. "But, Dr. Weizmann, we own London! It's already ours!" he said.

"But, Mr. Balfour," said Weizmann, "my people possessed the city of Jerusalem when London was a marsh."

The subject of Uganda never came up again.

In 1948, in accordance with United Nations Resolution 181, the independent Jewish State of Israel was established in the region of Palestine. This seemingly impossible dream of a Jewish homeland had become a reality—and the newly reestablished nation's first president was none other than Chaim Weizmann.[1]

The River of Impossibility

The "impossible dream" of a Jewish homeland was first given to Abraham around 2000 BC. That's when God promised Abraham, "I will make you into a great nation and I will bless you; I will make your name great, and you will be a blessing. I will bless those who bless you, and whoever curses you I will curse; and all peoples on earth will be blessed through you" (Gen. 12:2–3).

This "impossible dream" was handed down to Isaac and Jacob, then to Moses and Joshua. And now, as we come to Joshua 3, we find Joshua standing on the banks of what must have seemed to be the "river of impossibility," the river Jordan. As he looked out across that river to the land God had promised to Moses, Joshua must have been keenly aware of his own inadequacy, and the inadequacy of the people he led.

And here is where our lives intersect with Joshua's. You and I can testify to the fact that we have faced situations in our lives that seemed hopeless and impossible. Yet here we are! By God's grace, we made it! As we look back, we realize that He enabled us to cross our rivers of impossibility. The experience was difficult and painful—yet it stretched our character and increased our faith as we saw God enable us to:

- Obtain that seemingly unattainable graduate or post-graduate degree
- Survive that tragic loss

- Recover from that life-threatening illness
- Find joy again after that shattering betrayal
- Experience peace after that destructive family crisis
- Feel whole again after the devastation of being falsely accused

If you have spent much time on this earth, then you know God has brought you through challenges and struggles you thought you'd never survive. He has enabled you to cross a river of impossibility, and perhaps a number of such rivers. The experience of facing a river of impossibility will inevitably change us in one of two ways. Either the experience will make us stronger—or it will destroy us.

Some people break under the strain of life's "impossible" challenges. Some enter the waters of the river of impossibility, and they are overwhelmed by the flood and swept away by the current. But others, like Joshua, face their rivers of impossibility knowing that even though they are inadequate, God is supreme and more than adequate. They know He will lead them through the deep waters and safely to the other side. Those who trust in God will stand on the riverbank and look out over the waters, and where others see only impossibility, they will say, "What an opportunity to see God do something great in my life!"

It has been said that the difference between a live wire and a dead one is the connection. Those who are connected to God by faith will experience His power flowing through them. They will be live wires for God. Those who are not connected by faith will not receive God's power. So for God's live wires, *impossibility* is just another word for *opportunity*. For dead wires, an impossibility truly is a dead end.

God can use a river of impossibility to do great things in our lives—but Satan also uses rivers of impossibility. He will use them to discourage us, to silence our witness, to keep us from sharing Christ with others. He will continually try to get us to focus on our problems and obstacles instead of on the infinite power of God.

When you stand on the riverbank, as Joshua did, sometimes Satan will stand at your side, saying, "Look at that flood. Look how far it is to the other side. You can't cross that river! You'd be crazy to even try." When you hear the voice of discouragement and defeatism inside you, chances are it's the voice of Satan trying to turn you away from God's will for your life.

God has not given you a spirit of fear and defeatism. He longs to build your boldness and your faith. He wants you to cross those rivers so you can demonstrate His power to the world. He wants the people around you to see that one weak and inadequate person can literally do the impossible through faith in the God of infinite possibilities.

In Joshua 3, we see three crucial steps Joshua takes—three steps we must all take in order to cross the rivers of impossibility we face in our lives. Those steps are:

Step 1: Commissioning (verses 1-4)
Step 2: Consecration (verses 5-13)
Step 3: Completion (verses 14-17)

Let's look at each of these three important steps.

Step 1: Commissioning

As we saw in the previous chapter, Joshua had sent two spies into enemy territory, and those spies returned with a good report. As soon as Joshua heard the good report, he commissioned his people to cross over the river of impossibility, the river Jordan. Why was the river Jordan impossible to cross? Because of the time of year.

Later, in Joshua 4:19, we will see that these events took place on "the tenth day of the first month," the Hebrew month of Nisan, which corresponds to March–April on our calendar. Why is this timing significant?

Had the crossing of the Jordan taken place at any other time of year, cynics could have said, "Oh, the people could simply swim across at that time of year." But in the month of Nisan, the snows are melting on Mount Hermon and the waters of the Jordan are treacherously deep. The current is so fast that anyone foolish enough to step into the river would be swept away. As the chapter opens, we read:

> Early in the morning Joshua and all the Israelites set out from Shittim and went to the Jordan, where they camped before crossing over. After three days the officers went throughout the camp, giving orders to the people: "When you see the ark of the covenant of the LORD your God, and the priests, who are Levites, carrying it, you are to move out from your positions and follow it. Then you will know which way to go, since you have never been this way before. But keep a distance of about a thousand yards between you and the ark; do not go near it."
>
> (Josh. 3:1-4)

Joshua, through his officers, told the people that they were to follow the ark of the covenant and the Levite priests—and they were to walk straight toward the deep and rushing river.

What do you suppose the people said? I can imagine their response: "You want us to do *what?* You want us to walk into that river? Why now? Why not wait until summer, when the waters are not so deep? Joshua, you want us to do *what?*"

But Joshua had given the people their marching orders, which came straight from God. He told them when they were to go, what they were to do, whom they were to follow, and at what distance they should follow. As the people faced their river of impossibility, Joshua reminded them that they had been commissioned by God to cross that river and enter the land of promise.

And so it is with you and me. When we face our rivers of impossibility, we are tempted to forget that God Himself has commissioned us. We are tempted to say, "On top of everything else that's going on in my life, I don't need any more challenges. This really isn't a good time for me to go out of my way to witness for Christ. Someday, when I'm not feeling so stressed out, God can commission me to serve Him, but this just isn't a good time."

God is our Lord and we are His servants. It's not His job to adjust His plans to our convenience. When He commissions us and says "Go!" our job is to go.

I'm reminded of the story of a man who was under the conviction of the Holy Spirit. He felt God wanted him to witness to others about Jesus Christ. But he had plenty of excuses not to witness. Every time God gave him an opportunity to witness, he'd say, "Lord, is this really the right time? Is this really the right person?" And he would procrastinate until the opportunity was lost.

One day, he boarded an empty bus. There was not another soul on the bus except the driver. The man went all the way to the back and sat in the very last seat next to the window. At the next stop, a big, burly man boarded the bus. He looked at all the empty rows of seats, then he walked all the way to the back and sat next to the Christian man in the very last seat.

"Please, mister," the man said, "my life is a mess. I'm desperate. I want to know Jesus. Can you please tell me how I can be saved?"

The Christian man looked out the window and prayed, "Lord, is this really the right time?"

When God commissions us, it's the right time. It's the right purpose. It's His chosen opportunity. He has prepared this person and placed him or her in our path. It's up to us to obey.

God knew the Israelites would be afraid and filled with doubts. He understands and anticipates our fears and doubts as well. That's why He gave the Israelites—and us—the powerful visual symbol of the ark of the covenant going before them.

What was the ark? It was a sacred box built at God's command, as expressed in the vision of Moses on Mount Sinai (see Exod. 25:10–22). It contained:

- The stone tablets on which God had written the Ten Commandments—a reminder of God's law
- A jar of manna, the miraculous food God sent to feed the Hebrew people in the wilderness—a reminder of His provision
- The staff Moses raised at the parting of the Red Sea—a reminder of God's protection

Most important of all, the ark of the covenant represented the presence of God among His people. By sending the ark out in front of the people, God was symbolically saying to them, "I am going with you. I shall prepare the way for you and be your guide. As you cross this river of impossibility, you have nothing to fear and no reason to doubt because I am in your midst."

What a great God we have! He knew the people of Israel were going into the unknown. They were facing unfamiliar dangers. They were timid and hesitant. So He said to them, through the symbol of the ark, "I am going ahead of you—a thousand yards ahead of you, to be exact." For that is the distance spelled out in God's commission to the people: "Keep a distance of about a thousand yards between you and the ark" (Josh. 3:4).

God wants us to know that what was true in Joshua's day is still true today. Whenever we face our own rivers of impossibility, God says to us, "Don't be afraid. I am going ahead of you. Don't be terrified. I will make a way for you. Be strong. Be courageous. Follow Me."

Step 2: Consecrating

After the commissioning came the consecrating. We see this take place in the next few verses:

> Joshua told the people, "Consecrate yourselves, for tomorrow the LORD will do amazing things among you."
>
> Joshua said to the priests, "Take up the ark of the covenant and pass on ahead of the people." So they took it up and went ahead of them.
>
> And the LORD said to Joshua, "Today I will begin to exalt you in the eyes of all Israel, so they may know that I am with you as I was with Moses. Tell the priests who carry the ark of the covenant: 'When you reach the edge of the Jordan's waters, go and stand in the river.'"

Joshua said to the Israelites, "Come here and listen to the words of the LORD your God. This is how you will know that the living God is among you and that he will certainly drive out before you the Canaanites, Hittites, Hivites, Perizzites, Girgashites, Amorites and Jebusites. See, the ark of the covenant of the Lord of all the earth will go into the Jordan ahead of you. Now then, choose twelve men from the tribes of Israel, one from each tribe. And as soon as the priests who carry the ark of the LORD—the Lord of all the earth—set foot in the Jordan, its waters flowing downstream will be cut off and stand up in a heap."

(Josh. 3:5-13)

When the time came to cross the river of impossibility, Joshua did not say to the people, "Well, folks, we're about to cross over into the land of our enemies! It's time to sharpen your swords, polish your shields, and gear up for battle." Nor did he say, "Let's all do some calisthenics! You need to limber up those muscles. You're going for a swim today." No. He simply said, "Consecrate yourselves."

You may ask, "Why didn't Joshua prepare them for battle?" Answer: he did. He prepared them for *spiritual* battle. He prepared them for *supernatural* battle. He prepared them to fight a battle in the realm of the humanly impossible. You don't prepare for a spiritual battle by sharpening your sword or stretching your muscles. To be victorious over the river of impossibility in your life, you do not need powerful weapons or a clever strategy or a body like Arnold Schwarzenegger's. You simply need to be consecrated to God.

What does it mean to be consecrated to God? Consecration is the act of totally dedicating oneself to the service and worship of God. It is the act of setting oneself apart solely for God's own use. Consecration requires a complete surrendering of one's will. It requires being blameless before God. When you are consecrated, you cannot offer God any halfhearted commitment. Consecration is an all-or-nothing proposition.

Why does God allow rivers of impossibility in our lives? Is it so He can demonstrate His power in the midst of our trials? Yes—but I believe He wants to achieve even more than that. He also wants to bring us into a closer relationship with Himself. In other words, He wants us to consecrate ourselves 100 percent to Him. He wants us to examine our own lives and purge those sins we have tolerated and rationalized in ourselves. He wants us to cleanse ourselves of the idolatry and self-centeredness that have crept into our lives.

So, as you read these words, I would issue this challenge to you: if you feel you have been going through the motions of being a Christian, if you have not been an effective witness for God in your workplace or school or neighborhood, and if you have never led anyone to Christ in the mission field God has given you—ask yourself this question: *Am I consecrated to God?*

If you honestly have to answer no, then you're probably already aware of some changes you need to make in your life. You know there are idols you need to remove from your life. You know there are habits and sins you need to confess and repent. You know you are not fully surrendered to God's will. It's time to consecrate yourself.

And when you are fully consecrated, *watch out!* God is about to use you in a mighty way. You are about to become dangerous for God. You are about to deal a powerful blow to

Satan. You are about to cross that impossible, impassable river and set foot in the promised land of God's will for your life.

Step 3: Completion

The Israelites have gone through commissioning and consecrating. Now they are ready for Step 3: Completion. They need to complete the task God commissioned them to do, as we read in the next few verses:

> When the people broke camp to cross the Jordan, the priests carrying the ark of the covenant went ahead of them. Now the Jordan is at flood stage all during harvest. Yet as soon as the priests who carried the ark reached the Jordan and their feet touched the water's edge, the water from upstream stopped flowing. It piled up in a heap a great distance away, at a town called Adam in the vicinity of Zarethan, while the water flowing down to the Sea of the Arabah (the Salt Sea) was completely cut off. So the people crossed over opposite Jericho. The priests who carried the ark of the covenant of the LORD stood firm on dry ground in the middle of the Jordan, while all Israel passed by until the whole nation had completed the crossing on dry ground.
>
> (Josh. 3:14-17)

Imagine the thoughts that went through the minds of the Israelites—and especially the priests of Israel—as they approached the river. The priests, of course, were to be the first Israelites to step into the swirling, rushing waters. They were to carry the ark of the covenant. This is one of the greatest tests of faith found in the Old Testament. The priests had to ignore the evidence before their eyes and their own common sense. They had to do what God told them to do, trusting completely in His promises.

What do most of us do with the promises of God today? We underline them in our Bibles! Do we act on those promises? Do we step out in faith upon those promises? Do we dare great things for God, trusting in those promises? No!

What kind of faith is that? True faith is not just something we talk about. Faith is expressed in action. If we are not willing to *act* on God's promises, then how can we say we truly *believe* His promises?

Understand, I am not saying you should take wild and reckless gambles. Faith is not risking everything on a whim. Faith is acting boldly and courageously on the rock-solid foundation of God's reliable promises.

You may feel hesitant as you stand on the riverbank. You may tremble as you take that step of faith. That's all right. As long as you are willing to get your feet wet, God is pleased with your faith. Keep moving in the direction God is calling you. As long as you can look to your river of impossibility and say, "I am crossing this river in Jesus' name," God will be pleased with your faith.

Take Counsel of Your Faith, Not Your Fears

General George S. Patton Jr. commanded major military campaigns in North Africa, Sicily, France, and Germany during World War II. Once when General Patton was in Sicily, a fellow officer praised him for his bravery in battle. Patton is reported to have replied, "Sir, I am not a brave man." He went on to say he got sweaty palms at the sound of gunfire and the sight of war—but, he added, "I learned early in my life never to take counsel of my fears."

In late 1944, General Patton commanded the U.S. Third Army as it drove toward the Saar River region dividing France and Germany. During the predawn hours of November 8, Patton awoke to the earshattering sounds of a massive American artillery raining shells on German infantry positions. Patton thought it was a frightening sound, like the slamming of many doors in an empty house—and he couldn't help wondering about the fear the enemy must have felt as the long-dreaded Allied attack had finally come.

That morning, Patton recorded in his journal some thoughts that echoed what he had said earlier to a fellow officer in Sicily. He wrote that he was grateful for the fact that "I had never taken counsel of my fears," and "I thank God for His goodness to me."[2]

Patton was neither a fearless nor a flawless man. But whatever his personality flaws, he was a man who refused to listen to his fears. He persisted in doing his duty as he saw it—in spite of his sweating palms.

It doesn't require any bravery to do what you do not fear. If you do not feel fear, you can't demonstrate courage or faith. So if you are afraid to do what God calls you to do—*but you do it anyway*—be grateful for God's affirmation! Your Lord is proud of your courage. He's pleased with your obedient faith.

I'm sure the priests of Israel were filled with trepidation as they approached their river of impossibility—but they did not take counsel of their fears. They took counsel of their faith.

Living Memorials

As the Scriptures tell us, "The Jordan is at flood stage all during harvest. Yet as soon as the priests who carried the ark reached the Jordan and their feet touched the water's edge, the water from upstream stopped flowing. It piled up in a heap a great distance away. . . . So the people crossed over" (Josh. 3:15–16).

Cynics like to point out that there have been times in recorded history when the Jordan River has dried up so the riverbed was exposed. For example, history tells us that there was an earthquake on December 8, 1267, and the Jordan was dry for ten hours. Of course, that was in December, before the spring thaws had swelled the waters in the river. And on July 11, 1927, there was an earthquake that is said to have caused the Jordan to dry up for twenty-one hours. But that was in the summertime, long after the spring floods.[3]

There are no recorded instances of the Jordan River drying up during the flood time of March–April—except this account in Joshua. The river of impossibility became possible because of a supernatural intervention by the hand of God. The people of Israel crossed that river by faith in God. They did what couldn't be done because they trusted in His promises.

Once the Israelites reached the other side and set foot upon the promised land, they experienced a moment of realization: they could not go back. Once you begin walking by faith, there is no going back to the old way of life. There is no going back to being silent; you must speak out and witness. There is no going back to the spiritual wilderness; you must stay on the path that leads to the kingdom. There is no going back to fear, timidity, and mediocrity; you must go forth boldly and courageously.

Once you have crossed the river of impossibility, your eyes are open to the needs of the lost people all around you. You cannot ignore those people and pretend they have nothing to do with you. You realize God has placed them in your path for a reason, and you must share the hope that is within you.

My friend, God is calling you to face your river of impossibility, whatever it may be. He is calling you to take that step of faith, to get your feet wet, and to keep moving forward in reliance upon His promises. Your river and mine may be very different rivers, but God is calling us both to accept the challenge and cross over.

The story of crossing the Jordan River continues in Joshua 4. There God tells Joshua to set up a memorial to commemorate the miraculous crossing of the river of impossibility. He tells the Israelites to take twelve stones from the riverbed and carry them to the place where they camp for the night. There in the encampment, they are to build a monument of stones. And when their children ask what those twelve stones mean, the Israelites are to say that "the flow of the Jordan was cut off before the ark of the covenant of the LORD. When [the ark] crossed the Jordan, the waters of the Jordan were cut off. These stones are to be a memorial to the people of Israel forever" (Josh. 4:7).

Like those stones, our lives are to serve as living memorials to the power of God. When people ask us what our lives mean, we are to tell them, "By the sheer power and grace of God, I have crossed the river of impossibility. My life is a memorial to His grace forever."

God has commissioned you. So consecrate yourself, face your river of impossibility, and complete the work He has given you. Allow Him to make your life a living memorial to God.

4

You Want Me to Yield?

Joshua 5

Late at night on August 31, 1986, the Soviet passenger ship *Admiral Nakhimov* was sailing on the Black Sea with 888 passengers and 346 crew members aboard. The ship's pilot noticed that the *Admiral Nakhimov* was on a collision course with another ship and reported the situation to the captain, Vadim Markov. Captain Markov ordered the pilot to radio a warning to the other ship.

The message was received by the *Pyotr Vasev*, a massive Soviet freighter loaded with grain. Captain Viktor Tkachenko of the *Pyotr Vasev* radioed a reply: "Do not worry. We are aware of your course and we will miss each other." But he did nothing to change the ship's course.

Believing the problem had been resolved, Captain Markov of the *Admiral Nakhimov* went to his cabin to sleep. He left his second mate in charge of the ship.

Before long, however, the pilot of the *Admiral Nakhimov* realized the freighter had not changed course and the two ships were still heading toward a collision. He continued to send warnings to the other ship, but the freighter did not respond. The pilot begged the second mate to order a change of course, but the second mate replied that the captain had told him to maintain the ship's current heading.

Aboard the freighter *Pyotr Vasev*, the captain—who had not taken the situation seriously before—suddenly realized a collision truly was imminent. He ordered the ship's engines to full reverse. At the same time, the second mate of the *Admiral Nakhimov* also realized the two ships were about to collide, so he ordered a hard turn to port.

Both orders came too late.

Most of the passengers aboard the *Admiral Nakhimov* were sleeping. A few, however, were on the promenade deck, stargazing or dancing to the music of a live jazz band.

At 11:12 p.m., the prow of the freighter *Pyotr Vasev* knifed into the starboard side of the passenger ship, tearing a nine-hundred-square-foot gash in the hull. The cold waters of the Black Sea poured into the engine and boiler rooms, knocking out the ship's power. All over the *Admiral Nakhimov*, everything went dark as the ship listed to starboard and began taking on water. Terrified passengers got lost trying to find their way through pitch-black hallways.

The *Admiral Nakhimov* went down less than ten minutes after being struck. The ship never had a chance to launch its lifeboats. Although 811 people were eventually pulled alive from the oily water, 359 passengers and 64 crew members perished in the sinking. The freighter *Pyotr Vasev* suffered relatively little damage and helped rescue survivors from the water.

A commission of inquiry later determined that neither weather nor mechanical malfunction played a role in the disaster. Instead, the commission placed full blame for the accident on both Captain Markov of the *Admiral Nakhimov* and Captain Tkachenko of the freighter *Pyotr Vasev*. The cause of the deadly tragedy was sheer human pride—both captains had stubbornly refused to yield the right-of-way.[1]

We human beings hate to be told to yield. We don't like anyone getting ahead of us in line at the movie theater or the supermarket. We fly into a rage if someone cuts us off on the freeway. The idea of submitting to someone else or serving someone else makes us feel insulted and inferior. We demand to have our own way, and we refuse to yield to anyone—even God Himself.

The Bible Is a "Yield" Sign

What does this sign say to you? What are you supposed to do when you see this sign?

The yield sign tells drivers that when they enter an intersection, they must slow down and stop if necessary to give another driver the right-of-way. Drivers who fail to yield may be cited and fined up to several hundred dollars.

So the law takes yield signs seriously. We drivers, unfortunately, don't always do so. We are creatures of habit, and some of our driving habits can get us into trouble. If there is a yield sign along our daily drive to work or school, we sometimes become lax about obeying it. After a while, we don't even see it anymore. Then one day we get into trouble. We have an accident or we are pulled over by an officer. That's when we ask ourselves, *Why didn't I yield?*

The yield sign is there for a reason. When you obey it, you stay safe—and you help your fellow motorists stay safe. When you fail to yield, you risk your own safety and the safety of others. You may get away with failing to yield for a while, but sooner or later the failure to yield will get you into trouble.

In a very real sense, the Bible is a big yield sign. From cover to cover, from Genesis to Revelation, the message of the Bible is, "*Yield* to God!" If you want a meaningful life, yield to God. If you want to experience peace, joy, and contentment, yield to God. If you want to have an effective ministry and a fruitful witness, yield to God. If you want to experience victory in all the battles and struggles in your life, yield to God.

Yield to His will for your life. Yield to His commands and His gentle urging. Yield to the instructions in His Book. Yield the right to control your life to Him.

Let's be candid: yielding is not always easy, fashionable, or fun. But we will never be able to truly serve God and receive His blessings in our lives until we have fully yielded to Him.

"I'm Here to Take Over"

I once heard a story about a farmer and his wife who were traveling down a dirt road back in the days of the horse and buggy. As their horse pulled them along a narrow and dangerous stretch of road, the woman became anxious. The road hugged the side of a steep hill, and as she looked out over the side of the buggy, she could see a long, steep drop to a river far below. In a moment of panic, she snatched one of the reins from her husband's hand.

The husband, not wanting to frighten the horse, responded by gently offering his wife the other strap of the reins.

"Oh, no!" the woman protested. "I don't want both of the reins! I could never manage that animal by myself!"

"In that case," the husband said, "you must make a choice. Either take both reins—or let me take them. Two people cannot drive the same horse."

The farmer's argument convinced the frightened woman. Trusting in her husband's confidence and experience, she yielded control of the reins to him—and they safely reached their destination.

That is where we find the Israelites in Joshua 5. They had to learn to hand the reins of their nation completely over to God.

As the chapter opens, we find that word has spread across the land that the Lord has miraculously enabled the Israelites to cross the river. The kings of the Amorites and Canaanites are terrified of these former slaves who have entered their territory.

At this point, God instructs Joshua to circumcise the Israelite men. (In Genesis 17:10–14, God commanded His people to undergo the rite of circumcision as an outward sign of participation in Israel's covenant with God.) Because the Israelites have been wandering in the desert for forty years, all of the circumcised military men who came out of Egypt have died. The young men who were born during the Exodus in the desert are all uncircumcised. So, at God's command, Joshua ordered all the men of Israel to be circumcised and to remain in the camp until they were healed.

Then God said to Joshua, "Today I have rolled away the reproach of Egypt from you" (Josh. 5:9).

After the rite of circumcision, the Israelites celebrated the Passover. They also harvested grain from the land and ate unleavened bread. As soon as they began living off food from the promised land, the Lord stopped sending manna (the food He had miraculously provided to them in the wilderness). When the Israelites appropriated and consumed the produce of the promised land, they received a foretaste of God's coming victory.

The people of Israel camped on the plains near the city of Jericho. Joshua left the camp and looked out across the plain—and there he saw the city of Jericho, his military objective. The Scriptures do not tell us what Joshua's thoughts were at that moment. But I suspect that as he gazed upon the stone walls of that fortress, he probably thought about his people, who had never experienced war. Most of them had never even seen a fortified city. They had never attempted the conquest of such a formidable stronghold. Joshua may well have wondered if their faith and courage were up to the challenge.

As he stood there, thinking about the coming battle, he looked up and saw a man standing before him holding a gleaming sword. Joshua said to the man, "Are you for us or for our enemies?" (Josh. 5:13).

"Neither," the stranger replied, "but as commander of the army of the LORD I have now come" (5:14). In other words, this stranger told Joshua, "I'm not here to take sides. I'm here to take over."

Then Joshua fell on his face in reverence before the man and asked, "What message does my Lord have for his servant?" (5:14).

And the commander of the Lord's army said, "Take off your sandals, for the place where you are standing is holy" (5:15).

So Joshua fully yielded himself and removed his sandals.

God does not beg us or suggest to us that we yield. He does not offer us bribes or inducements to yield. He comes to us and says, "Yield." Period. He demands our yieldedness, and we must obey.

Why We Resist

Why does God demand that we yield ourselves to Him? For our good—and for His glory. Why, then, do we try so hard to wiggle out of yielding to Him? It's because our fallen will is bent toward rebellion, not obedience.

Amazingly, we resist God even though it is clear we can never know true peace, joy, and meaning until we are fully yielded to Him. And since our natural tendency is to rebel instead of yielding to God, He must often go to the trouble of taking away all other options. He must often make sure we have only the option to yield.

Let me tell you about a young couple in our church. A husband and wife felt God urging them to host a backyard Bible club at their home. Even though they felt this urging came from God, they resisted. And, from a purely human perspective, they had good reason to resist.

This couple had two children, a three-year-old and a two-month-old, and one on the way. Their children kept them very busy, and they didn't see how they could take on the time commitment of a backyard Bible club.

But as time went on, they realized that resisting God's urging was making them feel unhappy and dissatisfied. They knew what they had to do, so they yielded to God's urging. With the help of two other couples from church, they hosted the Bible club and invited kids from around the neighborhood. They put flyers in mailboxes, and they wondered if anyone would show up at the event.

The day of the first club event came—and more than fifty kids showed up! All of those children got to hear the good news of the love of Jesus. Moreover, as a result of that Bible club, nine moms from the neighborhood began attending a Bible study for young mothers. Why did this happen? Because one Christian couple overcame their resistance and made a decision to yield.

When you yield yourself to God, He will use you—guaranteed! He will prepare a ministry for you in your neighborhood, your workplace, or your campus. Yield to Him fully, holding nothing back. Yield to Him spiritually, giving Him all your worship and devotion. Yield to Him emotionally, making Him Lord of your joys and sorrows, your laughter and anger, your courage and fear. Yield to Him mentally, feeding your mind on the thoughts of God rather than the depraved and destructive ideas of this corrupt world. Yield to Him physically so your body will truly be His temple.

To be yielded is to be consecrated. As we saw in the previous chapter, consecration precedes conquest. Yielding precedes harvesting. When we are consecrated and yielded to God, He will bless us and make us victorious.

A Symbol of Yieldedness

How did the Israelites demonstrate their yieldedness to God? Perhaps the most striking symbol of their yieldedness was the act of physical circumcision, as recorded in Joshua 5:2-9. From a human perspective, this would seem to be the height of insanity. The men of Israel were about to go to war. So what did God tell them to do? He told them to perform a painful ritual that would leave the men physically incapacitated for days.

What was the point of this ritual? Why were religious rituals even necessary? Why should the people of Israel have had to carry out such seemingly pointless and painful acts? There is one answer to all of these questions. The people of Israel needed to yield to God.

It would be easy to yield to God if He never asked us to do anything difficult, costly, risky, or perplexing. If we yield only in matters where it is easy and pleasant to do God's will, we are not really yielding at all. We are truly yielding to God only when we are giving up our way to go God's way. If God is God, then we must yield even when it is hard to yield, even when it costs us everything, and even when God's will makes no sense to us.

What is God asking you to yield to Him? Something in your life may have become an idol. It has become a hindrance in your devotion to God. It might be a habit, a pastime, a goal, a career, a possession—and you clearly sense that God is urging you to yield that idol to Him.

The thing God wants you to yield might have no hold whatsoever on me, but it has dug its claws into your soul—and that is why God wants you to give it up to Him. At the same time, some possession or pursuit that might mean nothing to you could become a huge stumbling block in my life. Likewise God might urge you to yield something that would never be a problem in my life.

We all have our own idols. God's will for your life and mine is that we surrender those false gods in our lives and yield totally to Him.

A Reminder of Deliverance

At this point, you may be sensing a powerful resistance within. You might be thinking, *I don't want to give up my _____. Why should God ask me to give up something that means so much to me? It doesn't make sense!*

I don't know what God might be asking you to yield to Him. Only you can say whether God is prompting you or not. But I do know this: God will not ask anything of you that is more unreasonable or irrational than what He asked of Joshua and his fellow Israelites. On the eve of the greatest battle any of them had ever faced, God told them they needed to be circumcised. Joshua and his men yielded themselves totally to God in this area of their lives—and God gave them the victory.

If you are fully yielded to God, He will give *you* the victory.

Divine logic often seems unreasonable and irrational from a human perspective. That's because our perspective is limited while God's perspective is omniscient.

What was God's logic in ordering the men of Israel to be circumcised? What was the divine reason for physically incapacitating the men of Israel on the eve of battle? We might say it made no sense, but to God, it made perfect sense. Why? Because God didn't want His people to think they had won the battle in their own strength. He wanted them to know that God alone had given them the victory.

When God strips from us the last vestige of our personal strength, it may feel like a personal defeat—but in reality, it is the beginning of God's supernatural victory in our lives. As long as we are relying on our own power, our own strength, and our own resources, we are not relying on Him. He will not take away our free will, but He will allow us to flounder and fail in our own strength, if that is what we choose. But even while we rebelliously go our own way, He will continue to urge us to yield ourselves to Him so we can experience the victory He has planned for us.

The generation of Israelites who had crossed the Jordan into the promised land were born in the wilderness. Only a handful, such as Joshua and Caleb, remembered what it was like to live in slavery in Egypt. Only those few remembered what it was like to cross the dry bed of the Red Sea, and recalled what it looked like and how it felt to see the mighty Egyptian army swallowed up by its crashing waters.

The generation of Israelites who crossed into the promised land had never been circumcised. They had never received in their flesh the sign of the covenant God had made with Abraham. Moreover, this generation had never participated in the Passover.

The first Passover, of course, was in Egypt when the lamb was slaughtered and the blood was sprinkled on the doorposts. At the first Passover, the angel of the Lord *passed over* Israel and spared the firstborn sons (see Exod. 12).

The second Passover was observed at Mount Sinai (see Num. 9).

Now here, in Joshua 5, we see the third observance of the Passover—a reminder of God's mighty deliverance of His people from slavery in Egypt.

The first Passover in Egypt was God's act of delivering His people. The second Passover at Mount Sinai was a reminder of God's past deliverance. The third Passover at the camp on the plain of Jericho was both a reminder of God's past deliverance and a symbolic foreshadowing of an even greater deliverance—the deliverance from sin—that would come through Jesus the Messiah.

In much the same way, the sacrament of Holy Communion, the celebration of the Lord's Table, is both a reminder and a foreshadowing. It reminds us of God's act of deliverance and salvation through the death of Jesus the Messiah on the cross at Calvary. It is also a reminder that God continues to save His people in the present. And it foreshadows the day still to come when we all will gather around His table in heaven.

Christ in the Old Testament

What did it mean when Joshua encountered the commander of the heavenly army? Clearly, this is one of the most profound and exciting passages in all of Scripture.

Who was the stranger with the sword? Theologians generally agree that Joshua experienced a *theophany*, an appearance of the preincarnate Christ. The Man who stood before Joshua was not a ghost, nor was He a mirage. He was the Lord

Jesus in human form, appearing here in the Old Testament centuries before His incarnation at Bethlehem.

This same preincarnate Christ also appeared to Abraham under the great trees at Mamre (see Gen. 18). He appeared to Jacob at Peniel (see Gen. 32). He appeared to Moses at the burning bush (see Exod. 3). He appeared with His chariots of fire to Elisha and fought the Assyrians on Elisha's behalf (see 2 Kings 6). And here, in Joshua 5, the preincarnate Christ appears before Joshua with His sword drawn.

This stranger identifies himself as the "commander of the army of the LORD" (Josh. 5:14). In other words, Joshua is speaking to the commander of all the legions of God's angels. This is important for Joshua to understand, because he needs to know that when he and the people of Israel go up against the fortress that is Jericho, they do not go alone. The army of the Lord goes with them.

You and I also need to know that Jesus, the Son of God, the Commander of the army of the Lord, goes with us into all the battles of our lives. God is always ready to deploy the hosts of heaven on your behalf and mine. The moment you yield to the Lord's call upon your life, the moment you accept His call to be His missionary, His apostle, His ambassador, He will deploy His forces on your behalf.

So take the sandals off your feet. Yield yourself totally to the Lord of hosts, for the place He has sent you—your neighborhood, your workplace, your school—is holy ground.

Yield to Him your desires, your opinions, your comfort zone, your self-indulgence, your time and talent and treasure, your frustration and depression, your self-pity and bitterness. Yield it all to Him, and allow Him to send the armies of heaven to aid you and bring you victory.

The Scriptures also tell us that, when Satan rebelled and was cast out of heaven, one-third of the angelic hosts fell from heaven with him, swept away by Satan's mad rebellion (see Rev. 12:4). Two-thirds of all the angelic hosts remained loyal to God. They are ready and waiting to be deployed on behalf of yielded believers like you and me. This means that for every demon who wars against your soul, there are two of God's angels fighting on your behalf. As the writer to the Hebrews tells us, "Are not all angels ministering spirits sent to serve those who will inherit salvation?" (Heb. 1:14).

So, yield to your Commander in Chief. Go to Him and say, "Lord, I yield all I am and all I have to You. Take my yielded life and use it as You see fit."

Pastor and evangelist William Moses Tidwell (1879-1970) used to tell the story of a man who wanted to yield his life to God but couldn't bring himself to yield all. This man would come to Tidwell's evangelistic meetings, he would walk forward when Tidwell invited sinners to come forward and pray for salvation—and though the man prayed and prayed, he left the front of the church feeling discouraged and troubled.

"I'm not ready to yield all," he'd say.

One day, the man came forward to pray for salvation as he had done many times before. He prayed and prayed—and finally, he threw his hands in the air and shouted, "All right, Lord! I yield! Colt and all, Lord! Colt and all!"

When he shouted those strange words, the man's eyes lit up and his entire face beamed with joy. "Thank You, Lord!" he shouted. "At last, I know I'm saved!"

Someone asked the man, "What did you mean when you shouted, 'Colt and all, Lord'?"

The man explained that he was the owner of a stable of

racehorses. He had been sensing that God wanted him to give up his racehorses, because they were associated with the vice of gambling. The man was willing to give up racing and had already sold off most of his horses . . . but there was one fast colt that he had his eye on. That horse could outrun any other horse he had ever owned. "I just wanted to see that horse race one time," he explained. "So I told God I would give up the racing business—but first I wanted to see this colt run in one race. Though I prayed and prayed and tried to make a deal with God, I had no peace. I knew what God wanted from me. As long as I held on to the colt, He could not reign in my life. So finally I surrendered everything to Him—colt and all. And at that moment, I knew I was saved."[2]

What God said to that racehorse owner, He says to you and me. God cannot be Lord of anything in our lives until He is Lord of everything. When we fully yield to Him, He will come when we need Him—not to take sides, but to take over. He will prepare the hearts of our hearers, and He will give us the words to speak. He will bless our work and make us productive for Him. He will encourage us and meet our needs—and He will give us the victory.

5

You Want Me to Get with the Program?

Joshua 6

Even skeptics of the Bible admit that the destruction of the ancient fortress-city of Jericho was no myth. It is a historical fact, firmly attested to by archaeological evidence. Today, Jericho is a little village of twenty-five thousand people located in the West Bank. But that little village stands on the site of the ancient walled Canaanite city on the plain near the Jordan River—a city that was once a citadel of idolatry and military might. The origins of the city are shrouded in mystery; the evidence indicates that it was settled thousands of years before Christ.

The first scientific excavations of ancient Jericho were conducted by two German archaeologists, Ernst Sellin and Carl Watzinger, in 1907. Their discovery of Jericho's ruined fortress walls confirmed that the city had been destroyed in a way that was consistent with the Old Testament account. In fact, the walls appeared to have been destroyed so completely that the only earthly explanation was a powerful earthquake.[1]

The site was excavated again in the 1930s by British archaeologist John Garstang of the University of Liverpool. Professor Garstang found evidence of an intense fire that had consumed the city at the time that the walls collapsed. Structures built along the inside of the wall were burned to the ground, and a thick layer of ash, charcoal, and debris lay over everything. The destruction of the city and its walls was scientifically dated at somewhere between 1400 and 1600 BC.[2]

It's important to note that many other ancient Canaanite cities have been excavated in that same region. All of them appear to have been destroyed at around the same time as Jericho.

When we read this account in the book of Joshua, we are not reading a legend or a myth. We are reading the true account of how the Israelites of old overcame fear, committed themselves to God's program, and toppled the walls of Satan's domain.

The Divine Program

As we look at the story of Joshua and the battle of Jericho, we need to remember the parallels between Joshua's time and ours. Our culture is permeated by immorality, idolatry, and false religion. Atheism is not merely on the rise—it is on the march. Our society is encircled by enemies and terrorists who are committed to our destruction. We live in Jericho times.

Living as we do in such perilous times, it would be easy to allow ourselves to be controlled by fear. It's tempting to look upon the fortress of Satan's domain and say, "The enemy is too powerful. The walls of Satan's fortress are too strong. The forces controlled by Satan are overwhelming. It's hopeless. Why even try?"

That's the mind-set Satan wants us to have—a mind-set of fear, despair, and defeat. Our enemy knows he doesn't stand a chance against us if we live by faith in Jesus, our Commander in Chief. With confidence in our Lord, we can topple fortress walls of addiction, temptation, lust, hate, abuse, division, racism, and more. Trusting in Him, we can claim our neighborhoods, workplaces, marketplaces, and schools for Christ.

As Joshua 6 opens, we see a city under siege. The gates of Jericho are shut and tightly barred because the Canaanites within are terrified of the Israelites. No one goes in. No one goes out.

"The Lord says to Joshua, 'See, I have delivered Jericho into your hands, along with its king and its fighting men. March around the city once with all the armed men. Do this for six days. Have seven priests carry trumpets of rams' horns in front of the ark. On the seventh day, march around the city seven times, with the priests blowing the trumpets. When you hear them sound a long blast on the trumpets, have all the people give a loud shout; then the wall of the city will collapse, and the people will go up, every man straight in'" (Josh. 6:2–5).

So Joshua gives the order, and the people of Israel do as the Lord commands. As the people of Israel march around the city walls, Joshua reminds them, "Do not give a war cry, do not raise your voices, do not say a word until the day I tell you to shout. Then shout!" (Josh. 6:10).

The Canaanites within the city, who were already terrified of the Israelites, must have been beside themselves with
fear at this eerie spectacle. Day after day, these strange people
from across the river marched in silence around Jericho. There
were no war cries, there were no whispers—just a strange
and ominous silence.

And what did the Israelites think as they marched around
the city? They must have wondered what kind of battle plan
the Lord had in mind. They must have doubted the sanity of
Joshua himself. Yet, despite all their doubts and questions,
they did as the Lord commanded them through His servant
Joshua.

The English evangelist and preacher Dr. Alan Redpath,
who served as pastor of the Moody Church in Chicago in the
1950s, offered this profound insight into God's reasons for the
silent march at Jericho:

> God made the Israelites walk around the great fortification
> until within themselves they died to every hope of conquest
> unless God should mightily and miraculously intervene.
>
> Is there a Jericho in your experience? You are conscious
> that God has brought you along in the Christian life and
> manifested himself in blessing to you, but there is still some
> Jericho that haunts you. The greatest difficulty in the Chris-
> tian life is getting to the place where you are prepared to
> admit that the whole thing is too big for you and that the
> power of the enemy is too great for you. If your Jericho is to
> fall, then somehow God must bring it about.
>
> I believe that before God entrusts any of his people with
> a real measure of spiritual power, victory, and blessing, he
> brings them to a place where they have surveyed Jericho

for so long that they have come to see that its conquest is absolutely hopeless. . . . So as long as we think we can do it in our own strength alone, the miraculous resources of God cannot help us.[3]

As the nation of Israel marched in silence around Jericho, the people had come to the end of their own resources. They relied completely on the power of God. There is probably no point in Israel's history where the Israelites demonstrated more faith than right here in Joshua 6.

The previous generation of Israelites died in the wilderness because of their lack of faith. They murmured and complained against God instead of trusting Him, so they never got to see the promised land. But this new generation said no to fear and yes to faith. So, as I write these words, my prayer to God is, "Lord, may our generation in the twenty-first century be like the Joshua generation. May this generation have the faith and courage of Joshua's generation. And may this generation experience the same thrilling victory over Satan's stronghold."

Joshua's generation could well have asked, "Lord, You want us to do *what*? Penetrate the impenetrable fortress? Look at those massive walls! Listen to the taunting of the Canaanites! The city of Jericho has stood fast for centuries, perhaps thousands of years! Their weapons are more advanced than ours! Their armor is stronger than ours! They have a long warrior tradition while we are just a bunch of wandering ex-slaves!

"You want us to do *what*? Get with the program? Follow the divine strategy? Are You joking? What kind of military strategy is that? We're supposed to march around the walls of Jericho once a day in total silence for six days, then, on the seventh day, march around the city seven times, blow our trumpets, and shout! Lord, what is that supposed to accomplish? What do these silly rituals have to do with the price of beans in Babylon?

"First of all, Lord, if we do what You say, the whole nation of Israel will look ridiculous! And second, if those Canaanites on the city walls decide to lob a few spears at us, some of us could get killed! Lord, You want us to get with the divine program—but Your program makes no sense!"

The Scriptures do not tell us so, but I suspect that even Joshua himself must have had doubts. But Joshua did not act according to his doubts. He acted according to his faith. He responded with unquestioning obedience. He committed himself and his people to the divine program.

Unless faith is expressed in action and obedience, it's nothing but talk. The divine strategy made no sense according to human logic. But if God said, "Do it," then Joshua did it. He put his trust in God's wisdom, not human logic. He obeyed his Commander in Chief.

The Fortress of Fear

For thousands of years, one of the most vexing problems for military strategists has been how to conquer a fortress. The one feature that defines a fortress is its thick, impenetrable walls. All the great cities of ancient times were surrounded by walls of stone, and these walls not only defended the cities from attack, but also made a strong statement to all potential enemies: "Look upon these walls and despair! This fortress is invincible. Don't even think of attacking us!"

The great unconquerable Sumerian city of Uruk boasted

walls that were four stories high. The walls of the city of Babylon were flanked by towers and surrounded by moats; the city was never conquered by invaders, though it was eventually destroyed by revolt from within. The Hittites built their stone-walled cities on hills and mountains, so any would-be invader would have to scale the hillside as well as the walls.

To conquer an ancient fortress-city, an invader would have to lay siege to the city. In other words, the invaders was required to surround the city, cut off all commerce and traffic in and out, and keep the inhabitants of the fortress holed up inside for weeks, months, or even years. Laying siege to a walled fortress was usually a very difficult and expensive military operation requiring great patience and determination.

That's the kind of fortress Joshua and the Israelites faced on the plains of Jericho: Unyielding. Invulnerable. Invincible. The walled city of Jericho was a fortress of fear that defied all invaders.

It's interesting to compare the Old Testament story of Joshua and the battle of Jericho with the principles of spiritual warfare in the New Testament. You may be surprised to learn the name Joshua (in Hebrew, *Yehoshua*) is the equivalent of our Lord's name, Jesus (an Anglicized Greek form of *Yehoshua*, meaning "Jehovah saves"). So Joshua and Jesus are actually the same name.[4]

When Jesus spoke of establishing His church, He used imagery that suggested the kind of battle Joshua and the Israelites faced at the walled fortress of Jericho. In Matthew 16:18 (KJV), Jesus described His church as a mighty army that would lay siege to the fortress of hell itself, and He declared "the gates of hell shall not prevail" against it. The forces of hell are holed up behind walls and gates, but God and His church surround the walls of hell, and the gates of hell cannot withstand our assault. The victory of God's church is already assured.

The problem is that we often fail to realize we have already won the victory through Christ. We forget that our Lord has promised that the gates of hell will fall before us. We pull back in fear because we lack faith to believe our Lord's promise of total victory.

What is your Jericho? What is the towering, menacing obstacle that blocks your path to victory? What keeps you from claiming your mission field, your street, your office, or your campus for Christ? What is the fortress of fear that keeps you from carrying out the mission, the ministry, and the divine program God has given you?

Do feelings of inadequacy hold you hostage? Are you held back by some past hurt you are unwilling to forgive? Are you afraid of rejection? Are you afraid of what people will think of you if you speak up for Christ? Are you afraid of embarrassment or of making a mistake?

If we are honest with ourselves, we have to confess that all of these fears are rooted in disobedience. The Scriptures tell us again and again that we are not to be anxious or intimidated or fearful about speaking out for Christ. We are not to worry about what others think, and we should never be ashamed of the gospel of Christ. We should be quick to forgive and quick to seek forgiveness. So if any of these issues are holding us back, let's be honest with ourselves: our own disobedience hinders our witness.

Please understand, I would never minimize or trivialize the power of fear. I have experienced raw, heart-pounding fear on several occasions, and I know fear is one of the most demoralizing and shattering emotions in human experience. Our fears can become a prison more escape-proof than Alcatraz.

It's not a sin to experience a moment of fear when we face a genuine threat. But a pattern of habitual fear, worry, and timidity will rob us of our joy and our effectiveness for God. Our Lord wants to move us beyond fearfulness to faith in Him. He wants us to reach the full potential of our God-given gifts and abilities.

Fear and faith are like the opposite ends of a seesaw. When fear is up, faith is down. When faith is up, fear is down. The stronger our faith, the weaker and less significant our fears.

Courage is not the absence of fear. Rather, courage is fear managed by faith. When our emotions are ruled by faith, fear cannot control us. It's normal to experience fear in frightening situations, and only a fool has no fear in the face of real danger. But people of faith and courage do not let their fears determine their actions. As John Wayne once said, "Courage is being scared to death but saddling up anyway."

Just as Joshua and the Israelites overcame their fears as they marched around Jericho, we must say no to our fears and yes to God's program. Satan's fortress of fear is no match for our God.

Backward, Christian Soldiers

In previous eras of church history, Christians viewed themselves as God's soldiers, locked in spiritual combat. Followers of Christ saw themselves as warriors for Christ—and not in a metaphorical sense, but literally. They viewed themselves as part of a mighty army under the command of Jesus, their Commander in Chief. That is why Christians in times past sang bold, militaristic hymns such as "A Mighty Fortress

Is Our God," "Battle Hymn of the Republic," and "Onward, Christian Soldiers."

The mind-set of the twenty-first-century church was captured by an anonymous writer in this parody of "Onward, Christian Soldiers": "Backward Christian soldiers, fleeing from the fight . . ."[5] Those words were intended to provoke a smile—and a wince—of recognition. In all honesty, we must admit that there is a good deal of truth in those lines. The church today does seem timid, afraid, and scattered in retreat before our enemy. We are divided one from another, and we show all too little love.

What is God's answer? Simple: "Get with My program." And what is God's program? "Trust in Me. Study the Word I have given you. Spend time with Me in prayer, worship, meditation, and intimate fellowship. Get to know Me. Learn to recognize My voice when I speak quietly to you within your spirit. Become sensitive to My guidance and direction in your life."

When we get with God's program and develop a true intimacy with Him, we will truly know what the prophet Isaiah meant when he said, "Whether you turn to the right or to the left, your ears will hear a voice behind you, saying, 'This is the way; walk in it' " (Isa. 30:21).

For some of us, getting with God's program means we need to overcome our shyness, our fear of what others will think of us. We need to speak up more. We need to stop letting golden opportunities for witnessing slip through our fingers. We need more boldness and more courage to seize the opportunities God brings our way.

But for others of us, getting with God's program means we need to speak less and love more. It means we need to learn to stop barging blindly into every situation and preaching a fire-and-brimstone sermon to everyone we meet. Sometimes God calls us to listen and to love and to keep our mouths shut for a while. Some people need to experience the *love* of God, as expressed through the sensitive caring of His people, before they will respond to the *Word* of God. Every human soul is unique, and we should not apply a one-size-fits-all approach to everyone around us.

I know a little bit about the Middle Eastern tempera-ment, so I think I can identify with Joshua and the Israel-ite people. And I think that one of the hardest challenges the Israelites faced in getting with God's program was that God commanded them to be *silent*. God said, in effect, "No talking—for a week!" Telling people from the Middle East not to talk is like telling a pig to fly. Those Israelites had to march around the walls of Jericho without talking, day after day after day. By the third or fourth day, the silence must have been killing them!

Moreover, the Israelite people were not one big homoge-neous group. The Israelite nation was made up of twelve tribes, and those tribes were always quarreling with one another. To get with God's program, they had to stop bickering and start marching in unison. They had to stop complaining and argu-ing and demanding their own way. The fact that Joshua got all of these tribal people to march around the city as one unit was a miracle in itself.

Do you remember what Jesus prayed for in the Upper Room, just hours before going to the cross? He asked the Fa-ther "that all of them [all Christian believers] may be one, Father, just as you are in me and I am in you. May they also be in us so that the world may believe that you have sent me"

(John 17:21). In other words, Jesus prayed that we would be unified and undivided, because our unity would serve as a witness to the world of the Lord Jesus' relationship of unity with the Father.

Jesus prayed that you and I and all other Christians would be united in prayer, united in worship and fellowship, united in mission and purpose, united in tithing and giving, united in serving and witnessing, and united in our love for one another. That is God's program for the church. That is how we are to reach out and claim our neighborhoods, workplaces, and schools for Christ. If we truly believe in His program and practice Christian love and unity, we can transform our cities, our nation, and our world. I believe that with every ounce of my being.

Faith in Action

General George Patton had an unusual method of selecting officers for promotion. In *General Patton's Principles for Life and Leadership*, Porter B. Williamson reports that the general would take a group of officers out behind a warehouse and say, "Men, I want you to dig a trench on that spot. Dig it eight feet long, three feet wide, and six inches deep." Then he would leave the officers alone to carry out their work.

What the men didn't know was that Patton would slip into the warehouse and eavesdrop on their conversation while they worked. Some would complain, "This is grunt work. It's demeaning to make an officer dig trenches!" Others would say, "The old man must be nuts! We've got mechanized equipment that could dig this trench in two minutes!" Still others would say, "Why six inches? What is he going to do with such a shallow trench?"

But there was almost always one man who would say, "Who cares what the old so-and-so wants to do with this trench? The sooner we get the job done, the sooner we can get out of here!" And that was invariably the man Patton selected for promotion. A leader who could take orders without questioning or complaint was exactly the kind of leader who was fit to give orders.[6]

God is looking for men, women, and young people who are willing to get with His program. He is looking for people who put their faith to work by acting in obedience to His will. When we act in obedience, God acts in power. When we act in obedience, God manifests His purpose in our lives. When we do the possible, God takes care of the impossible. When we get with His program and carry out His strategy, He gives us the victory.

Get with His program, and He will deliver Jericho into your hands. Fortress walls will topple before you. Hearts will melt. The enemy will flee. Miracles will take place right before your eyes. God will do what only He can do.

Down through the years, many generals, military planners, and military historians have studied the book of Joshua, seeking the secret of Joshua's victory over Jericho. They have tried to understand Joshua's strategy. They have asked, "Where was Joshua schooled in the military arts? Where did his soldiers obtain their armor and weaponry? Certainly, there must be some hidden meaning to the story of the siege of Jericho."

But there is no secret, no hidden meaning. The biblical text says what it means and means what it says. Joshua's victory over Jericho was not won by superior military strategy or superior armament. The Israelites won because they obeyed the plan of God. They won because Joshua and the people of Israel got with God's program.

A Curse and a Blessing

The closing verses of Joshua 6 tell us of the destruction of the city of Jericho. On the seventh day, the people of Israel got up at daybreak and marched around the city seven times and then, as God had commanded, the priests blew the trumpets and the people gave a loud shout. At the sound of that shout, the walls of the city collapsed and the Israelites entered the city unopposed. They conquered the city in the name of the Lord.

Joshua remembered and honored the promise that the two spies had made to Rahab the prostitute. She and her household were spared, but the Israelites burned the city and everything in it. Nothing was left but a layer of ash, charcoal, and blackened debris—which is exactly what archaeologist John Garstang found when he excavated the site of Jericho in the 1930s.

After the destruction of the city, Joshua pronounced a solemn oath: "Cursed before the LORD is the man who undertakes to rebuild this city, Jericho: At the cost of his firstborn son will he lay its foundations; at the cost of his youngest will he set up its gates" (Josh. 6:26).

You may wonder, if Joshua made such an oath, why does the town of Jericho still exist today on the West Bank and Israel? The answer is found in the book of 1 Kings. There we read: "In Ahab's time, Hiel of Bethel rebuilt Jericho. He laid its foundations at the cost of his firstborn son Abiram, and he set up its gates at the cost of his youngest son Segub, in accordance with the word of the LORD spoken by Joshua son of Nun" (16:34).

Hiel of Bethel pursued his own program and rebuilt Jericho according to his own selfish will—and he and his sons paid the price. Yet God in His sovereign wisdom took the rebuilt city of Jericho and transformed that city into a symbol of His grace in the New Testament.

Do you remember the Lord's parable of the good Samaritan? Jesus began that story by saying, "A man was going down from Jerusalem to Jericho . . ." (Luke 10:30). In this story, the road to Jericho becomes a place where the words "love your neighbor" are demonstrated in a practical, tangible way.

And in Luke 19, we see Jesus entering the city of Jericho, where He encounters a despised but wealthy tax collector named Zacchaeus. Jesus reaches out to this notorious sinner and transforms his life, so that Zacchaeus exclaims, "Look, Lord! Here and now I give half of my possessions to the poor, and if I have cheated anybody out of anything, I will pay back four times the amount" (v. 8).

And Jesus replies, "Today salvation has come to this house. . . . For the Son of Man came to seek and to save what was lost" (Luke 19:9–10). Imagine: Yehoshua-Jesus brought salvation to the very city where Yehoshua-Joshua brought destruction!

Jericho is also the place where Jesus healed several blind men, including Bartimaeus (see Matt. 20:29–34; Mark 10:46–52; and Luke 18:35–43). The city that was once a fortress of fear became a holy place of grace and healing as Jesus walked its streets.

May we, as followers of Jesus Christ, pattern our lives after Jesus and Joshua. Instead of pursuing our own programs and asking God to bless our plans, let's get with God's program. When we obediently submit ourselves to His program and carry out His strategy, He will banish our fears, give us the victory, and make us Christlike agents of His healing grace.

6

You Want Me to Learn from My Mistakes?

Joshua 7–8

Ｈow much damage can one traitor do?

Single-handedly, a traitor named Clyde Lee Conrad could have caused the defeat of America in a World War III nuclear scenario. Conrad was a retired army sergeant living in Germany who sold top secret information to Soviet bloc spies in the 1970s and 1980s, earning well over $1 million for his treachery. He also recruited other army retirees and enlisted men, paying them for intelligence information that he resold to the enemy at a profit.

Conrad's most damaging act of betrayal was the sale of the General Defense Plan, NATO's top secret plans for responding to a Soviet attack. The plans Conrad sold to the Communists described in detail exactly what the United States and NATO would do if the Soviets invaded Western Europe—where military units would be positioned, how a defense would be mounted, and the nature of all NATO's strengths and weaknesses. With the sale of those plans, Conrad gave the Soviets the entire game plan for a World War III.

Conrad was arrested in 1988 and convicted of espionage and treason in 1990. He was sentenced to life in prison, and he died of a heart attack in 1998 while confined in a German jail cell. He was fifty years old.

The German judge who presided over Conrad's trial described how this one man's crime could have led to utter defeat for the West—and the deaths of millions of people in a nuclear holocaust. "If war had broken out between NATO and the Warsaw Pact," the judge concluded, "the West would have faced certain defeat. NATO would have quickly been forced to choose between capitulation or the use of nuclear weapons on German territory. Conrad's treason had doomed the Federal Republic [of Germany] to become a nuclear battlefield."[1]

So how much damage can one traitor do? A single traitor can bring defeat down upon his entire nation. It happened before in Old Testament times at a place called Ai.

The Ambush at Ai

We now come to what is undoubtedly the most heartbreaking and tragic section of the entire book of Joshua. The people of Israel have just entered the promised land and, through faith in the power of God, they have won an amazing victory over the Canaanite foe. But immediately after this thrilling triumph, the Israelites are about to suffer a devastating setback. And one man's moral and spiritual weakness will result in death and defeat for his nation, shame for his family, and the tragic end of his own life.

This is the story of how God's people were ambushed from without and betrayed from within.

You probably know what it feels like to be ambushed or betrayed. Few experiences are more emotionally devastating than that. You are going about your life when a sudden disaster strikes. You feel as if a trapdoor has opened beneath your feet. You learn that for weeks or months, while you thought life was going along smoothly, someone you counted on has been betraying you, deceiving you, ruining your reputation, and undermining the very foundation of your life.

Out of the blue, your spouse tells you, "I'm leaving you. I want a divorce."

Or your business partner is arrested and you discover that he has been secretly, systematically plundering the company you've built—and you're left with nothing.

Or the son or daughter who always seemed to walk with the Lord now gives you the shocking news: "I'm pregnant"; "I'm addicted to drugs"; "I don't believe in God anymore."

You cry out to God, "Why, Lord? Why is this happening?" And you have been ambushed. You have gone from victory to a sudden and unexpected defeat. That is what happened to the people of Israel after the victory at Jericho, when they went up against the next Canaanite stronghold, the city of Ai.

The catastrophe at Ai in Joshua 7 was foreshadowed in Joshua 6, shortly before the conquest of Jericho began. There, Joshua told the Israelites what they should do with any "devoted things," objects of silver and gold the Canaanites used in their pagan religious ceremonies:

> Keep away from the devoted things, so that you will not bring about your own destruction by taking any of them.

Otherwise you will make the camp of Israel liable to destruction and bring trouble on it. All the silver and gold and the
articles of bronze and iron are sacred to the LORD and must
go into his treasury.

(Josh. 6:18–19)

In the opening verses of Joshua 7, we come upon these ominous words: "But the Israelites acted unfaithfully in regard to
the devoted things; Achan son of Carmi, the son of Zimri, the
son of Zerah, of the tribe of Judah, took some of them. So the
LORD's anger burned against Israel" (Josh. 7:1).

Who acted unfaithfully? "The Israelites," the Scriptures tell
us. How many Israelites were actually involved in the theft of
the devoted objects? One man, "Achan son of Carmi, the son
of Zimri, the son of Zerah, of the tribe of Judah." One man
committed a sin that would prove destructive to the entire
nation of Israel.

The account tells us that Joshua sent spies into Ai, just as he
had sent spies into Jericho. The spies returned with a glowing
report. The city of Ai would be a pushover. "Not all the people
will have to go up against Ai," the spies reported. "Send two
or three thousand men to take it and do not weary all the
people, for only a few men are there" (Josh. 7:3). Israel's over-
confidence led directly to an ambush:

So about three thousand men went up; but they were routed
by the men of Ai, who killed about thirty-six of them. They
chased the Israelites from the city gate as far as the stone
quarries and struck them down on the slopes. At this the
hearts of the people melted and became like water.

(Josh. 7:4–5)

Joshua was devastated by the defeat of Israel at Ai. He tore his clothes and fell upon his face before the ark of the covenant. The elders of the nation joined Joshua, covering their heads with dust as a sign of mourning.

And Joshua cried out,

> Sovereign LORD, why did you ever bring this people across the Jordan to deliver us into the hands of the Amorites to destroy us? If only we had been content to stay on the other side of the Jordan! O Lord, what can I say, now that Israel has been routed by its enemies? The Canaanites and the other people of the country will hear about this and they will surround us and wipe out our name from the earth.
>
> (Josh. 7:7-9)

The Lord told Joshua to stand up—then He told Joshua the reason for Israel's ambush and defeat:

> Israel has sinned; they have violated my covenant, which I commanded them to keep. They have taken some of the devoted things; they have stolen, they have lied, they have put them with their own possessions. That is why the Israelites cannot stand against their enemies; they turn their backs and run because they have been made liable to destruction. I will not be with you anymore unless you destroy whatever among you is devoted to destruction.
>
> Go, consecrate the people. Tell them, "Consecrate yourselves in preparation for tomorrow; for this is what the LORD, the God of Israel, says: That which is devoted is among you, O Israel. You cannot stand against your enemies until you remove it."
>
> (Josh. 7:11-13)

So the next morning, Joshua had all of the Israelites come forward and present themselves before the Lord, tribe by tribe, clan by clan, family by family, and ultimately man by man. Through this process of elimination, Joshua zeroed in on Achan son of Carmi, the son of Zimri, the son of Zerah, of the tribe of Judah. And Achan confessed:

> It is true! I have sinned against the LORD, the God of Israel. This is what I have done: When I saw in the plunder a beautiful robe from Babylonia, two hundred shekels of silver and a wedge of gold weighing fifty shekels, I coveted them and took them. They are hidden in the ground inside my tent, with the silver underneath.
>
> (Josh. 7:20–21)

Joshua sent messengers to search Achan's tent. They brought out the stolen items and spread them on the ground before all of Israel, in the sight of the Lord. And Joshua said to Achan, "Why have you brought this trouble on us? The LORD will bring trouble on you today" (Josh. 7:25).

And Achan was executed by stoning, and everything he owned was destroyed in a place called the Valley of Achor (the Hebrew word *achor* means "trouble"). A large pile of rocks was erected over the site of Achan's execution (see Josh. 7:26).

Responding to Trials and Tragedy

Some people look at Bible passages like this one and draw the conclusion that when bad things happen to believers, it is always a judgment from God. That's not true. Trials and tragedies are simply a part of living in a fallen world. God's people sometimes suffer through no fault of their own.

However, it is also true that God often uses adversity in our lives to make us aware of our need for change. Sometimes when we suffer, our suffering is a consequence of a wrong or sinful choice we have made. So when we encounter a trial of adversity, we need to examine our own lives and ask ourselves, *Is God trying to get my attention? Are these problems the result of sin in my life?*

We need to pray, "Lord, what are You trying to tell me? What are You trying to teach me? I don't want to miss any of the lessons You have for me, so please help me to hear and understand what You are saying to me through this trial."

When Israel suffered a setback at Ai, Joshua immediately responded by casting himself down before God in prayer. He wanted to understand the reason for this mysterious and devastating setback. He wanted to root out the sin that had resulted in death and defeat for the Israelite people. So he, together with the elders of the nation of Israel, went to God with their faces on the ground and sought an answer to the troubling question of their defeat.

Joshua is a great role model for how we as Christians should respond to trials and tragedy. All too often, when we suffer a defeat or loss, our response is to complain: "God, it's not fair! This shouldn't be happening! I shouldn't have to suffer like this!" We turn a blind eye to the very thing God wants us to confront. We rationalize our sins and refuse to give them up. We deny our sins instead of confessing them and repenting of them. We resist God as He tugs at our consciences. We sweep our dirty secrets under the rug instead of allowing God to clean house.

Do you recall what Joshua said when he fell on his face before God? "Sovereign Lord, why did you ever bring this people across the Jordan to deliver us into the hands of the Amorites to destroy us?" (Josh. 7:7). It was commendable for Joshua to go to God with his questions—but do you not detect a note of accusation in that question? Joshua is saying, "Lord, how could You do that to us? You've let us down! Did You bring us all this way just to hand us over to our enemies? Lord, You owe us an explanation!"

This is a very human response on Joshua's part. It is often our nature to question God whenever we face a loss or defeat. I have done so. I'm sure you have as well. We think God has let us down, and so we blame Him for our troubles.

But God did not let Israel down. The nation of Israel was betrayed from within. Someone in the camp broke the covenant. Someone disobeyed God's injunction. Someone stole what belonged to God. The result of that disobedience was defeat—not merely for one man, but for the entire nation of Israel. Innocent men died and the battle was lost because of one man's betrayal and hidden sin.

It's important to understand that the seeds of Israel's defeat at Ai were planted at the very moment of Israel's triumph over Jericho. This is a scenario we all can relate to as Christians. When we are struggling with problems in our lives, when we are facing rivers of impossibility and fortresses of fear, we recognize our need for God. We become prayer warriors. We purge sin from our lives and we earnestly seek to live godly lives.

So God in His mercy answers our prayers. He delivers us and leads us into triumph over our adversity. We are ecstatic, joyful, and grateful to God—for a while.

But that euphoric sense of gratitude doesn't last long. We become comfortable and perhaps a little smug. Things are going well now. We think we don't need God's help at the moment. We think we don't need to pray as much as we once did. And if we start returning to those former bad habits, we figure He will understand. He'll overlook a few sins. No need to confess or repent, because life is pretty good.

Perhaps that was the attitude of Achan. He had marched with the army of Israel, and he had seen the walls of Jericho destroyed by trumpet blasts and a shout. This was the moment of Israel's triumph. Achan was overjoyed and grateful to God.

But as Achan plundered one of the Canaanite storehouses, something caught his eye. He saw a beautiful robe from Babylonia, two hundred shekels of shining silver, and a gleaming wedge of gold. In the moment of Israel's triumph, Achan coveted the things that belonged to God—and he took them. At the very moment that the rest of the nation of Israel was celebrating victory, Achan was stealing and ensuring a future defeat.

Perhaps you can identify with Achan. Perhaps, when life has been good and problems have been few, you lost your sense of gratitude. Your prayers became sporadic. You lost touch with God. And sins that were once unthinkable soon became habitual.

You experienced a defeat. You experienced an ambush. And, like Joshua, you found yourself crying out to the Lord, "Why, Lord? Why is this happening to me?"

A New Beginning

Defeat does not have to be the end of your story. You have fallen down, but God wants to lift you up. You've been knocked out of action, but God wants to restore you to usefulness for Him. There are three stages to every experience of defeat and restoration. These stages follow one another as day follows night.

1. Carelessness
2. Calamity
3. Closure

Let's take a closer look at each.

Stage 1: Carelessness

One of the greatest dangers facing Christians today is that they underestimate the destructive power of sin. They say, "I know what the Bible says about sin—but that doesn't apply to my situation. After all, I'm saved by God's grace. Jesus died on the cross for my sins and I have liberty in Him. Oh, I know I shouldn't do some of the things I do—but God in His grace overlooks my sins. I'm not worried about any consequences."

Underneath this lax attitude toward sin is a burning, raging conscience. Though we may try to justify or rationalize our disobedience, we know deep down God does not overlook sin. We may become casual and careless about sin, but God never does. And only a fool takes God's grace for granted.

That's why the Scriptures tell us, "Work out your salvation with fear and trembling" (Phil. 2:12). The sin of disobedience is serious—but equally serious is the sin of presumption. We should never take the grace, mercy, and goodness of God for granted. Our attitude toward God's grace should be one of grateful obedience, not presumptuous sin. Let me suggest to you some areas in which we often rationalize our disobedience:

Disobedience in our finances. God said the tithe belongs to the Lord, and He will pour out His blessing on us if we are obedient to Him in our finances:

> "Bring the whole tithe into the storehouse, that there may be food in my house. Test me in this," says the LORD Almighty, "and see if I will not throw open the floodgates of heaven and pour out so much blessing that you will not have room enough for it."
>
> (Mal. 3:10)

Yet we are quick to rationalize a choice to spend God's tithes on ourselves. According to George Barna, director of the Barna Group, Ltd., tithing has become "uncommon" in churches today. He writes,

> For a number of years, The Barna Group has . . . been following the practice of "tithing," which is donating at least ten percent of one's income. . . . Very few Americans tithed in 2004. Only 4 percent gave such an amount to churches alone; just 6 percent gave to either churches or to a combination of churches and parachurch ministries.[2]

Our giving to God should be punctual, regular, and cheerful. Under the Old Testament, tithing was a requirement of the law. But under the New Testament, the principle of Christian giving is based on love and gratitude to God. We are no longer under the law, which demanded that 10 percent of our earnings go to God. We are under the new covenant, under which we acknowledge that everything we are and everything we own belongs to God, and we gratefully give a portion back to Him. As the apostle Paul said, "Each man should give what he has decided in his heart to give, not reluctantly or under compulsion, for God loves a cheerful giver" (2 Cor. 9:7).

Disobedience in our ethical behavior. Your integrity and ethical behavior are essential to your witness in this sinful and dying world. If your behavior as a Christian is no different from the way the world behaves, what difference does it make? What example do you set for the people around you that would make them eager and hungry to know more about your faith?

Many Christians explain away their unethical behavior, saying, "You have to cut a few corners to compete in the business world today. Integrity is old-fashioned. In today's economy, you do what it takes to survive."

Well, I won't kid you. There may be times when you will have to pay a price to maintain your integrity. Maintaining your Christian ethical standards could cost you a sale, a promotion, or even your career. But your willingness to pay the price for maintaining your integrity could be the very thing that impacts the people around you for Jesus Christ.

I recently had a conversation with a brilliant young Christian businessman. He had been with his company for fourteen years and was highly regarded in his field. But he had reached an invisible ceiling and was stuck there, unable to obtain a promotion. When he asked his superiors why other, less qualified people were being promoted ahead of him, they gave him vague excuses and told him he needed to be patient.

Finally, one of his coworkers told him candidly that the word around the office was that this young Christian executive was being kept out of upper management because he would not lie or cheat the customers. He was paying a price because of his reputation for integrity. This was a hard thing for this young man to hear, but he told me that his one consolation was he now knew he had a reputation for honesty around the office. Even if he didn't get a promotion, he knew he had a witness.

Integrity isn't cheap, but it's worth every cent it costs you. If you are willing to trade your integrity for mere money and status, then you are to be pitied. As Jesus said, "What good is it for a man to gain the whole world, yet forfeit his soul?" (Mark 8:36).

Disobedience in our sexual and moral behavior. King David stood on his rooftop and saw a beautiful woman bathing below. He could have turned away—but instead, he stayed, he looked, and he lusted. That moment of lust led to his undoing. He followed the urgings of his lust into the depths of adultery and murder. He arranged for the death of another man and took that man's wife as his own.

When David's sin was revealed, God, speaking through the prophet Nathan, told David, "Now, therefore, the sword will never depart from your house, because you despised me and took the wife of Uriah the Hittite to be your own" (2 Sam. 12:10). This prediction was fulfilled when David's beloved son Absalom led a revolt against David and plunged the kingdom of Israel into civil war.

And it all began with a moment of lust.

What kinds of thoughts occupy the secret places of your mind? How do you use your computer when no one else is looking? What kinds of programs do you watch on television? What kinds of movies do you view? What kinds of books do you read? What kinds of thoughts do you have about other people in your neighborhood, at your office, or on your campus? Do you think about how to reach them for Christ—or would you be ashamed of your thoughts if they were revealed to the world?

The Carelessness of Achan. God does not take a lax attitude toward sin, and neither should we. You may be able to justify or rationalize your disobedience for a while, but sooner or later the consequences of sin will catch up to you. You may think, *It's just a little sin. It doesn't hurt anyone.* Yet it was just a little bite from the forbidden fruit that doomed Adam's race to death. And it was just a robe, a few pieces of silver, and a bar of gold that Achan stole, yet it cost Israel the victory at Ai. Sin is like a pebble cast into a pond, and you never know how far its ripples will spread.

The seventeenth-century English preacher Jeremiah Burroughs put it well when he warned, "Take heed of secret sins. They will undo thee if loved and maintained: one moth may spoil the garment; one leak may drown the ship; a penknife stab can kill a man as well as a sword."[3]

One of the great dangers of secret sin is that it breeds complacency within us. When we act in disobedience to the Word of God, and God does not immediately punish us for our disobedience, we tend to misinterpret God's patience and grace. We think, *God's not displeased at all! It looks as if I got away with it!* So one sin leads to another and soon becomes a habit of sin.

But God is not pleased. He is waiting for us to come to our senses and repent, but we should not mistake His kindness for laxness. The consequences of our sin are accruing, and the bill will eventually come due.

Who was this man Achan? Can we dismiss him as nothing more than a thief with a lust for silver and gold? Or is he more like us than we want to admit? Perhaps he stole because he was fearful and insecure, and he thought that possessing a few items of silver and gold would enable him to store up provisions for the future and better provide for his family. We should ask ourselves, *In what ways am I like Achan? And what can I learn from his tragic story?*

Remember what we learned in the previous chapter: fear and faith are like the two ends of a seesaw. When fear is up, faith is down. When faith is up, fear is down. I think Achan was probably a fearful man. He felt insecure about the future. He didn't trust in the constancy of God's provision. He worried about whether he would have enough money to provide for his family.

Achan's level of fear was high—so his level of faith was low. As a result, at the moment of Israel's triumph in Jericho, Achan was unable to trust in God's provision. Even though God provided manna for the Israelites to eat during their forty years in the wilderness, Achan did not trust God to provide. Even though God enabled Israel to cross the river of impossibility, Achan did not trust God to deliver.

It was as if Achan were saying, "Yes, I know of all the great things God has done in the past, but how do I know He will continue to do great things in the future? What if He forgets us? What if He abandons us? How do I know I can trust God in the future?"

This is deadly thinking. If you think God did great things in the past but may not take care of you in the future, you have no trust in His faithfulness. Your fearful and faithless attitude will lead you into carelessness about sin. That's where

Achan's carelessness led him—straight into the second stage: calamity.

Stage 2: Calamity

Achan's careless disobedience brought disaster not only to himself, but to his family and his entire community. We think our secret sins affect no one but ourselves. We think we can hoard our tithes and offerings and it won't matter to God or to the church. We think, *God doesn't need my money*. And that's true, He doesn't. But we need to give!

God tells us in His Word,

> "Will a man rob God? Yet you rob me. But you ask, 'How do we rob you?' In tithes and offerings. You are under a curse—the whole nation of you—because you are robbing me. Bring the whole tithe into the storehouse, that there may be food in my house. Test me in this," says the LORD Almighty, "and see if I will not throw open the floodgates of heaven and pour out so much blessing that you will not have room enough for it." (Mal. 3:8-10)

You might think, *Well, Michael Youssef is just trying to manipulate people into giving money to his ministry*. I assure you, I am talking about this subject only because I am committed to teaching everything taught in God's Word. He says that those who withhold the tithe are robbing Him, so if you carry this principle to its logical conclusion, people who withhold their tithes from God are driving to church in stolen cars, sitting in church wearing stolen clothes, and sitting down to a Sunday supper of stolen food.

God will be patient with us for a while—but only for a while. And when His patience comes to an end—*calamity!*

And when we cry out to God in the midst of our calamity, He will say to us, "Remember what I told you in My Word." Carelessness inevitably leads to calamity.

God gave Israel the victory by leading the people across the river of impossibility. He gave them the victory when, at the sound of trumpets and a shout, He threw down the walls of Jericho. God wants His people to be victorious. He wants us to go from one glorious victory to the next, from one great height to an even greater height, from one mountaintop to an even higher mountaintop.

God takes no pleasure in our setbacks and defeats. Calamity is not His will for our lives. He wants us to experience the joy of abundant living. He wants us to move ever deeper into an intimate experience with Him. He is pleased to use us to touch the lives of others. He places people in our path so we will reach out to them and share the good news of Jesus Christ.

My friend, do not be careless with sin, for carelessness leads to calamity, and calamity will mar your testimony. Don't let Satan lull you into becoming lax with sin. Examine yourself. Put an end to your denials and rationalizations. Purge the hidden sin from your life, and keep your witness for Christ pure and untarnished. Do that, and you will be ready for the next stage: closure.

Stage 3: Closure

In Book VIII of his *Confessions*, Saint Augustine wrote:

At the beginning of my youth, I begged You to make me virtuous, and I said, "Give me chastity and self-control—only not yet." For I feared that You would hear me too soon, and that You would quickly cure me of the disease of my sinful desires. I wanted to satisfy those desires, not extinguish them. (author's paraphrase)[4]

Perhaps you can identify with Augustine's confession. Perhaps you have wanted to satisfy sinful desires, not extinguish them. You know that those sins are wrong and dangerous to you and the people around you. You would like God to purge those sins from your life—but not yet.

So you say, "Lord, I definitely plan to get rid of those sins someday. But there's plenty of time. No need to rush things."

That attitude of carelessness toward sin is keeping you from being an effective witness for Christ. It is keeping you from experiencing victory in your life. It is an Achan-like attitude destined to lead you to calamity unless you can find the closure God wants you to experience.

What kind of closure am I talking about? Repentance. This means you turn to God and say, "Lord, I want to be fully obedient to You. I want You to extract all the hidden sin out of my life—not 'someday,' but *now*. Lord, I turn from my sin. I choose full obedience to You. Seal this commitment and give me the power to keep it."

Don't make the mistake of thinking you can repent of your sin once and for all and all temptation will go away. You will be tempted. You may fail a time or two. But God knows if your desire to repent is sincere. When you fall, He will lift you up and tell you, "Try again, My child."

In the Old Testament book of Hosea, there is an amazing passage where God speaks of Israel as a wife who has betrayed the relationship by committing adultery. In that passage, God says:

"I will punish her for the days
   she burned incense to the Baals;
she decked herself with rings and jewelry,
   and went after her lovers,
   but me she forgot," declares the LORD. *(Hos. 2:13)*

At first glance, the Lord's words seem angry. He speaks of punishing Israel for her infidelity. But He goes on to declare His gracious love for Israel:

Therefore I am now going to allure her;
   I will lead her into the desert
   and speak tenderly to her.
There I will give her back her vineyards,
   and will make the Valley of Achor a door of hope.
There she will sing as in the days of her youth,
   as in the day she came up out of Egypt. (Hos. 2:14–15)

God says He will make the Valley of Achor a door of hope. What is the Valley of Achor? As we've seen, it's the place where Achan was executed by stoning. The name of the place means "trouble." And God, through the prophet Hosea, tells us that this place where Achan confessed his sin, then paid the consequences of his sin, shall become a door of hope.

When we confess our sins and purge disobedience from our lives, we pass through a door of hope. We experience a new beginning in our lives. It's the beginning of a new ministry, the beginning of a new testimony, the beginning of a new life of faithfulness to God.

Don't Ignore the Warning Signs

As I write these words, it has been only a matter of months since my brother went to be with the Lord at the age of sixty-eight. He was a brilliant economist and one of the godliest men I've ever known. He was instrumental in leading me to the Lord. I love him and miss him dearly.

Two years before his death, I learned he had been having physical symptoms that sounded like the warning signs of colon cancer. Knowing him as I do, I pleaded with him to get medical attention for these symptoms. But because he was a man of a certain mind-set, he dismissed the symptoms and refused to see a doctor.

Finally, the symptoms became so serious he could no longer ignore them. He went into the hospital and the doctors performed surgery, but by that time the cancer had run rampant in his body. There was no hope of saving him.

My friend, please hear me out. Disobedience to God is a deadly spiritual cancer. Do not ignore the warning signs. Do not dismiss these symptoms. Do not rationalize the hidden sin eating away at your spiritual life and your relationship with God.

Yes, you can ignore the symptoms for a while, but the disease continues its deadly progression. There is only one way to deal with it, and that is to expel it from your life. You cannot afford to be careless with sin any more than you can afford to be careless with cancer. Purge this malignancy now before it robs you of your spiritual vitality.

Then, when you have cleansed your life, prepare yourself for the victory God will give you. Walk through the door of hope that opens before you.

Israel was defeated at Ai because of Achan's sin. But the defeat at Ai was not the end of Israel's story. After Achan confessed his sin, God wrote a new chapter in the story of Israel. Joshua 7 is the story of Achan's sin and Israel's defeat. But Joshua 8 is the story of how, after the sin was purged, God told Joshua, "Do not be afraid; do not be discouraged. Take the whole army with you, and go up and attack Ai. For I have delivered into your hands the king of Ai, his people, his city and his land" (Josh. 8:1).

So Joshua and the army of Israel ambushed the army of Ai and conquered the city. Then Joshua built an altar to the God of Israel on Mount Ebal, and he offered sacrifices upon the altar. There he read the words of the Law of Moses before all the assembled people of Israel, and Israel reaffirmed its covenant with the Lord.

Carelessness with sin leads to calamity. But, like Israel, we can move from calamity to closure through repenting and purging our sin. Once we have moved to closure with God, we can step through the door of hope—and walk through the gates of victory.

7

You Want Me to Learn to Pray for Discernment?

Joshua 9

I once spoke with a group of young Christian professional people in the Middle East. We were talking about some of the challenges they faced in the business world, and one of them said, "In business, lying is so commonplace that you can never know for sure whether someone is telling the truth." Others in the group nodded and agreed that deception was the order of the day in their business environment.

I turned to a young professional woman in the group and asked, "Don't business relationships depend on trust? A contract or verbal agreement means nothing if you can't trust the other person's word. How can you do business in such an environment?"

The young woman replied, "I constantly pray for discernment and wisdom."

You may say, "Well, that problem is unique to a certain culture in a distant land. Here in America, we have a different view of honesty and integrity. And while we've had our share of business and political scandals, we can generally trust one another. And the one place where we need not worry about being deceived is in the churches of America."

If that is your view, let me share with you some sobering facts. During a four-year period in the United States, churchgoing folks were bilked out of $450 million by scam artists who posed as church members. These con men joined churches and became functioning members of congregations. They spoke the Christian language. They could recite Scripture and stand up and pray like any real believer. They played their parts well—but they cheated many churchgoers out of their life savings through phony investment scams and pyramid schemes. In fact, they preyed upon the feeling of trust that Christians naturally have for one another in the body of Christ.[1]

Deceivers and their schemes are all around us. And let's face it: Christians are especially susceptible to deception precisely because of our Christian love and grace. We know that God calls us to a depth of intimate community and fellowship in the church that transcends any worldly relationship. The original Greek New Testament has a word for this intense degree of fellowship: *koinonia*. Out of our righteous desire for *koinonia* fellowship, we are sometimes overly trusting. We need to recognize that there is no virtue in being gullible. Again and again, in both the Old and the New Testaments, God tells His people to be wise and not to be deceived.

As we come to Joshua 9, we will see how even a wise leader like Joshua could be duped. Whenever we face a key decision in our lives, our first response must be to pray to God for wisdom and discernment—and to pray against the spirit of deception.

The Scheme of the Gibeonites

As Joshua 9 opens, we see that word of Israel's victories over Jericho and Ai has spread far and wide, from the hill country to the Mediterranean coast and as far north as Lebanon. The kings of the pagan nations gather to make war against Israel—all, that is, except a clan of Hivites who live in the town of Gibeon. Instead of war, these pagan Gibeonites resort to deception:

> They went as a delegation whose donkeys were loaded with worn-out sacks and old wineskins, cracked and mended. The men put worn and patched sandals on their feet and wore old clothes. All the bread of their food supply was dry and moldy. Then they went to Joshua in the camp at Gilgal and said to him and the men of Israel, "We have come from a distant country; make a treaty with us."
>
> The men of Israel said to the Hivites, "But perhaps you live near us. How then can we make a treaty with you?"
>
> "We are your servants," they said to Joshua.
>
> But Joshua asked, "Who are you and where do you come from?"
>
> They answered: "Your servants have come from a very distant country because of the fame of the LORD your God. For we have heard reports of him: all that he did in Egypt, and all that he did to the two kings of the Amorites east of the Jordan—Sihon king of Heshbon, and Og king of Bashan, who reigned in Ashtaroth. And our elders and all those living in our country said to us, 'Take provisions for your journey; go and meet them and say to them, "We

are your servants; make a treaty with us."' This bread of
ours was warm when we packed it at home on the day we
left to come to you. But now see how dry and moldy it is.
And these wineskins that we filled were new, but see how
cracked they are. And our clothes and sandals are worn out
by the very long journey."

(Josh. 9:4-13)

At this point in the story, we read this tragic statement:
"The men of Israel sampled their provisions but did not inquire of the LORD. Then Joshua made a treaty of peace with
them to let them live, and the leaders of the assembly ratified
it by oath" (Josh. 9:14-15).

Those words jump out at us from the page as if they were
written in neon lights: Joshua and the men of Israel "sampled
their provisions but did not inquire of the LORD"! And because
they left God out of their deliberations and did not ask Him
for wisdom and discernment, the Israelites took the Gibeonite
bait.

Here we see the danger of following our own human wisdom and trusting in appearances.

Vulnerable to Deception

Why did Joshua fail to ask the Lord for wisdom and discernment? If we want to understand the lessons of this story
for our own lives, we need to place it in context. Joshua's
error in judgment does not take place in a vacuum. There is
a reason why he and the elders of Israel were vulnerable to
deception.

You will recall that at the end of Joshua 8, the army of Israel had conquered the city of Ai. In gratitude to God, Joshua

built an altar on Mount Ebal. He offered sacrifices, read the words of the Law to the people, and reaffirmed Israel's covenant with the Lord. In short, Joshua and the people of Israel had just experienced a powerful revival. They had rededicated themselves to God and to obedience to His Word. They had gone through a mountaintop experience.

And that was a dangerous time for Joshua and Israel.

We should always be especially watchful immediately after a spiritual victory. The spiritual euphoria of a "mountaintop experience" with God can make us vulnerable to spiritual deception. These are Satan's opportunities to fool us, and many a Christian has fallen prey to Satan's traps immediately after a spiritual high point.

As Paul wrote to the Corinthians, "If you think you are standing firm, be careful that you don't fall!" (1 Cor. 10:12). In other words, whenever you think you have it made, watch out! That's precisely the time you are the most vulnerable to Satan's deceptions and schemes. The account goes on to tell us:

> Three days after they made the treaty with the Gibeonites, the Israelites heard that they were neighbors, living near them. So the Israelites set out and on the third day came to their cities: Gibeon, Kephirah, Beeroth and Kiriath Jearim. But the Israelites did not attack them, because the leaders of the assembly had sworn an oath to them by the LORD, the God of Israel.
>
> (Josh. 9:16–18)

As you can imagine, the people of Israel were not happy with their leaders. In fact, they grumbled and complained against the elders of the nation. But Israel's leaders replied:

> We have given [the Gibeonites] our oath by the LORD, the God of Israel, and we cannot touch them now. This is what we will do to them: We will let them live, so that [God's wrath] will not fall on us for breaking the oath we swore to them. . . . But let them be woodcutters and water carriers for the entire community.
>
> (Josh. 9:19–21)

Then Joshua confronted the Gibeonites about their deception, and he told them, "You are now under a curse: You will never cease to serve as woodcutters and water carriers for the house of my God" (Josh. 9:23).

And the Gibeonites explained that they had fooled Israel for the sake of self-preservation. They knew that God had commanded Israel to take over the promised land and wipe out all of its inhabitants. Reasoning that it was better to sacrifice their integrity than lose their lives, the Gibeonites lied. "We are now in your hands," they said. "Do to us whatever seems good and right to you" (Josh. 9:25).

An Unwise Oath

If you go to Israel and visit the Arab village of Al-Jib, north of Jerusalem, you will be standing on the site of ancient Gibeon. The ancient city was excavated from 1956 to 1962 by James B. Pritchard, an archaeologist from the University of Pennsylvania. Pritchard and his team uncovered many structures, wine cellars, water conduits, and artifacts corresponding with the biblical accounts regarding the city of Gibeon. They even excavated a large pool that matches the biblical description of the pool of Gibeon mentioned in 2 Samuel 2:13. Hebrew inscriptions found in the ruins confirm that the site is that of the biblical city of Gibeon.[2]

Once again, secular archaeology confirms that the Old Testament record is a reliable historical account. The lessons of this biblical text come to us from actual events. And one of the most important insights we can learn from this story is the lesson stated in 1 Samuel 16:7: "The LORD does not look at the things man looks at. Man looks at the outward appearance, but the LORD looks at the heart."

That is why we need to pray for wisdom and discernment from God. Whenever we face a crucial decision, we need to see the situation from God's perspective, not a merely human perspective.

Joshua's vow to the Gibeonites, which he sealed with an oath before God, would later prove to have consequences for the nation of Israel. In 2 Samuel 21, Israel endured three years of famine and David went to God and asked the Lord why the nation was suffering and starving. And the Lord told David that it was because King Saul had slaughtered many of the Gibeonite people in violation of the oath that Joshua had made.

It was an oath Joshua would not have made if he had prayed for discernment. Joshua and the elders made that oath because they looked upon the outward appearance. They failed to ask God what was at the heart of the matter.

Dangerous Mountaintops

How should we apply the lesson of Joshua 9 to our lives?

You probably know what it's like to have a spiritual high. Sometimes a "mountaintop experience" literally takes place on a mountaintop—for example, at a Christian retreat or conference in the mountains. You spend a few days surrounded by the beauty of God's creation and you listen to Christian speakers who challenge you to a deeper walk with God. You respond, you rededicate your life to Christ, and you come away feeling that you have turned a corner in your Christian experience. You'll never go back to being the person you once were.

Then, within a few days of returning to your everyday life, you find that Satan attacks, hitting you with one temptation after another. Or you experience a series of devastating trials and setbacks. Or you are beset by frustration and opposition. And you wonder, *What happened? When I was on the mountaintop, I felt so close to God! I was on top of the world! My faith seemed so real, and my relationship with God was never stronger. Now I feel I'm at the lowest point in my entire spiritual life!*

Or perhaps you have a different kind of spiritual high. You are involved in an outreach program in your community and have seen God use you in a great way as you've shared your testimony with others. They have responded by giving their lives to Christ. You've been helping to meet human needs, sharing your time and resources with the poor and disadvantaged. You feel that God has reaffirmed your call to be His apostle wherever you may go. You feel closer to Him than you have ever felt before.

And that's when Satan ambushes you and traps you in one of his deceptive schemes. Suddenly, you learn a Christian leader you looked up to is a fraud. Or you find that your reputation is under attack and your motives are being questioned by other people. Or you find yourself unexpectedly tempted in some area of your life—what the Bible calls "the lust of the flesh, and the lust of the eyes, and the pride of life" (1 John 2:16 KJV). And you wonder, *Why is that suddenly such a problem in my life when it never was before?*

My friend, don't be surprised if you suddenly experience opposition and deception at the very moment you begin to be effective for Jesus Christ. Satan is watching for those moments, and he wants to quench God's power in our lives. The moment we begin to breathe deeply of the Spirit of God, Satan will try to smother us. That is a fact of life to which virtually every mature Christian can attest, and which the Old and New Testaments underscore for us.

When Jesus began His messianic ministry of preaching, healing, and casting out demons, He soon faced a barrage of opposition. Three groups that had traditionally quarreled and struggled with one another suddenly united against their common enemy, Jesus of Nazareth. These groups were the Pharisees, the Sadducees, and the Herodians. These factions remained united in their hostility against Jesus throughout His public ministry.

Whenever you become serious about exercising your calling and your life's mission, whenever you speak out for God, whenever you claim your workplace or campus or neighborhood for Him, you can expect opposition to arise. The moment you become effective for Christ is the moment Satan begins working overtime to deceive you and make you fall. All hell will break loose! And even other Christians—people you counted on as brothers and sisters and friends—will misunderstand you, misjudge you, and undermine you.

That's why you must know how to pray for wisdom and discernment when you are besieged by Satan and his schemes.

Twisting Scripture

The Gibeonites knew God had commanded the Israelites to invade Canaan and wipe out all its inhabitants. They knew their cities stood directly in the path of the Israelite onslaught—and they couldn't defeat God's people.

So they resorted to deception—and it was a diabolically clever scheme. They pretended to be something they were not and succeeded in fooling Joshua and the people of Israel. You may ask, "How did the Gibeonites know God commanded Israel to wipe out the inhabitants of the land of Canaan?"

The Scriptures do not tell us how, but somehow word had reached them of what God had said to Israel. In Deuteronomy 20, God had told the Israelites they should wipe out any enemies who made war against them, plunder the nearby cities, make peace treaties with the distant cities, and take over the promised land. The Gibeonites knew God's command to Israel, and they quoted it verbatim.

There is a lesson in this account we can apply to our lives today: the people who are the most deceptive are often the very ones who can quote the Bible as well as you can. They will use the Scriptures to silence you, to confuse you, to tie you in knots, and to keep you from speaking the truth.

Deceivers will say such things as, "Doesn't the Bible say God is love? Aren't you supposed to love people unconditionally, regardless of what they say or do or believe? Then how can you say someone is not going to heaven if he or she doesn't believe in Jesus Christ? Aren't you being judgmental to say such a thing? Doesn't the Bible say, 'Do not judge, and you will not be judged'? Why are you judging people who don't believe that Jesus Christ is the only way? Why do you say people are 'sinning' just because they don't live up to *your* moral standards?"

Such people will quote the Bible out of context and twist its meaning to intimidate us into silence. If you want to know the best way to respond to someone who uses deceptive tactics to sidetrack your witness for Christ, read John 4, the story of our Lord's encounter with the Samaritan woman.

When Jesus was at Jacob's well in Samaria, a woman came to draw water. Jesus spoke to her, and in her responses, she cleverly tried to throw Him off-track. She used the same kinds of verbal trickery and diversion people use today. But Jesus wasn't taken in by her tactics.

The woman said, in effect, "Jews have no dealings with Samaritans." Jesus let that pass. She said, "Our traditions say thus and so." He ignored it. She said, "The Jews and Samaritans have different belief systems." He refused to take the bait and get caught up in a debate over whose belief system was right.

Jesus was focused on one thing: the woman's desperate spiritual need. She was living a sinful life, and more than anything in the world, she needed to experience repentance, forgiveness, and a new life of faith. He kept bringing the conversation back to the woman's personal need. He forced her to reexamine her life and to recognize that she had no peace with God. He evaded all her clever attempts to change the subject—until at last she surrendered.

Jesus lived in total dependence upon God the Father.

Through prayer, He continually sought the mind, the wisdom, and the discernment of God. So the woman's deceptive schemes did not work on Him.

If Joshua and the leaders of the Israelite people had gone to the Lord and sought His counsel, wisdom, and discernment, God would have shown them that the Gibeonites were not what they claimed to be. He would have shown them that the Gibeonites used a twisted knowledge of God's commands to seduce them and lead them away from the truth. That is what deceivers always do with God's Word.

A Teakettle of Truth, an Ocean of Lies

When I gave my life to Jesus Christ in 1964, a friend of mine accepted Christ at the same time. We immediately began to witness to everyone we met. We didn't need to take a course on evangelism or apologetics. We simply told people what Jesus had done in our lives.

Now, everyone in the neighborhood knew what a mischievous young man I was before my conversion. All I had to do was tell people how Jesus had changed my life, and people would say, "Wow, really? That's amazing!"

My friend and I both started going to the places where we used to hang out. We would talk to our unsaved friends and acquaintances, and we'd tell them about the change Jesus had brought about in our lives. My friend and I were equally intense in our commitment to witnessing and evangelism.

But as time passed, my friend's passion for sharing Christ started to wane. He began to slip back into his old patterns. He went back to hanging out with his worldly friends. His behavior changed. His speech changed. He stopped talking to people about Jesus. And within six months, he was back in the world, full blast.

What happened to this young man? What happened to his intense passion for sharing Jesus Christ with other people? You might think his evangelistic fervor waned because he was ridiculed or persecuted. But no, the people he and I witnessed to were generally polite. They'd listen to us, ask us questions, and talk to us about our beliefs.

And one other thing—they quoted Scripture. When we told them something Jesus had said, they turned right around and countered with another verse from the Bible. Of course, the Scriptures they used were twisted and wrenched out of context. They used the Bible to deceive my friend.

So, while he was trying unsuccessfully to win them to faith in Christ, they were winning him back to the world.

Dr. Donald Grey Barnhouse told a story from the life of Joseph Duveen, the influential London art dealer of the early twentieth century. Duveen once took his daughter to the beach, but she refused to go into the water because she feared the ocean was too cold. He was sure that once she went into the water she would enjoy it, but he was unable to coax her into giving it a try.

So Duveen built a fire on the beach, put a teakettle over the fire, and heated the water in the kettle until it whistled and steamed. He took the steaming teakettle to the water's edge and made sure his daughter watched him as he poured the hot water into the ocean. His plan worked. The little girl went into the water and enjoyed playing in the waves for the rest of the afternoon.[3]

The trick Joseph Duveen played on his little girl may seem harmless, but this is exactly how the world often deceives us. False teachers often pour a small amount of comforting truth into an ocean of falsehoods. Then we go wading in it. We don't even suspect that we have been lured into a sea of lies. While we are splashing about in wave after wave of Satan's deception, we are being drawn away from our love for God and our mission of being ambassadors for Jesus Christ.

As you read the story of Joshua and the Gibeonites, you stumble onto a troubling realization: Joshua had his suspicions. There was a check in his spirit as he listened to the Gibeonites' story. When the Gibeonites claimed that they had come from a distant city, Joshua had his soldiers check their donkeys, look in their bags, and examine their wineskins. He doubted their story—but when he examined the evidence, everything seemed to confirm their claims. It seemed to check out because Joshua was looking at the situation from a human perspective.

As the apostle James tells us, "If any of you lacks wisdom, he should ask God, who gives generously to all without finding fault, and it will be given to him. . . . You do not have, because you do not ask God" (James 1:5; 4:2). Notice, the apostle does not say that God *may* give it to you. He says that God *will* give it to you—generously and in abundance! That is a promise.

One of the most dangerous things any Christian can say is, "I can handle this." I have heard Christians say those tragic words again and again, and I cannot think of one time it has turned out for the best. I have heard Christians say, "I can handle this relationship, even though God's Word says it is wrong." I have heard Christians say, "I can handle this temptation," or, "I can handle this decision without any advice, without any help."

Those who take a go-it-alone attitude, who resist all offers of help or Christian counsel, or who resist God's prescription for their problem, inevitably come to grief. They always seem to experience remorse and regret. They always seem to say, at some point, "If only I had listened. If only I had asked for help. If only I had asked God for wisdom and discernment. But now it's too late."

A friend once asked me, "What are your strengths?" I said, "I have none." He said, "Well, what are your weaknesses?" I said, "Every area of my life." That is not false modesty. That is the absolute truth. May God protect me from ever speaking those fateful words, "I can handle it." I know Satan would love nothing more than for me to revel in my "strengths." That is why, along with the apostle Paul, I choose to revel only in my weaknesses (see 2 Cor. 12:9). And that is why you and I must continually pray for discernment to resist the deceitfulness of sin.

Only prayer can open our eyes to Satan's subtle deception. Only prayer can give us the wisdom to see through the flattering words and manipulative schemes of the ungodly. Only prayer will protect us from a false sense of security we feel during mountaintop experiences. That's why Jesus taught us to pray, "And lead us not into temptation, but deliver us from the evil one" (Matt. 6:13).

Without God's wisdom and discernment, we can make the most disastrous decisions imaginable and end up with failed marriages, failed ministries, failed business ventures, and failed lives.

We can't handle this life in our own strength. Our enemy

is smarter than we are, and his deceptions are too subtle and persuasive. We need to daily and continually ask God to deliver us from the evil one.

Keep Your Integrity and Keep Your Word

A final comment about keeping your word: it's important to notice Joshua's response to the Gibeonites after they had deceived him. When the deception of the Gibeonites was revealed, many of the Israelites wanted to take their revenge against the Gibeonites. Even though Joshua and the leaders of the nation had made a covenant with the Gibeonites, many of the Israelites reasoned that a covenant based on deception should not be binding.

But Joshua and the leaders of Israel acted with integrity. Even though they had been deceived and even humiliated, they kept their word to the Gibeonites. Why? Because they did not want to bring disgrace upon God and His people by violating their oath. Joshua punished the Gibeonites for their deception, but he also kept his word to them.

Joshua's actions are instructive to us all. Let me give you an example.

In 1 Corinthians 7, the apostle Paul gives the church an injunction about marriage between a believing and nonbelieving spouse. He says that if the nonbelieving spouse chooses to leave the marriage, then the Christian spouse is not bound to the marriage. But if the nonbelieving spouse is willing to remain married to the believer, the believer should honor his or her wedding vows and keep the marriage intact. After all, Paul says, "How do you know, wife, whether you will save your husband? Or, how do you know, husband, whether you will save your wife?" (1 Cor. 7:16).

A believing spouse might say, "But I wasn't a Christian when I made that vow. I didn't know I would one day accept Christ and then go to church alone, pray alone, and raise my children in the faith without any help from my spouse. I didn't know how hard my life would be as a Christian married to a nonbeliever."

That's true. But by keeping your wedding vows (even though you made those vows as a nonbeliever, not understanding what they would ultimately mean), you are demonstrating a level of faithfulness, integrity, and commitment that brings honor and glory to God.

You may have taken some wrong turns in your life because you did not ask God for wisdom and discernment. You may have made decisions based on deception. You were deceived either by some other person or by Satan, or perhaps you were even self-deceived. You cannot undo the past, but you can start right now making good decisions for your life. It is always a good decision to honor your vows and commitments.

God does not want you to remain mired in failure. He does not want you to live in bitterness toward those who have deceived you. He does not want you to live in a state of constant regret. Ask God for forgiveness; He will give it to you. Ask God for wisdom; He will give that to you as well.

We human beings think we know everything. So we come to a fork in the road and we must make a choice—and we sense the Holy Spirit trying to get our attention, urging us to pause and pray about a decision we are about to make. And that's not our nature, is it? We tend to treat prayer not as the first order of business, but as a last resort. So our response to God, all too often, is, "You want me to do *what?* Learn to pray for discernment?"

But if we turn to God for wisdom, He will provide it generously and abundantly—and we will live rich, satisfying, and
victorious lives. So learn from the example of Joshua, including his mistake. Learn to pray for wisdom and discernment,
and God will bring joy out of your sorrow, light out of your
darkness, and gladness out of your sadness.

8

You Want Me to Claim the Total Victory?

Joshua 10–12

General Ambrose Burnside served as a Union army general in the Civil War. His distinctive facial hair—a bushy fringe that started in front of his ears, curved down around his jowls, and joined up with his mustache—combined with his name, Burnside, inspired the style of whiskers we now call "sideburns." During the war, General Burnside led successful military campaigns in North Carolina and Tennessee—and he should have easily won a major victory at Petersburg, Virginia. Instead, Burnside became known as the architect of one of the worst defeats the Union side suffered during the Civil War.

Here's what happened: by mid-1864, the war between the Union and the Confederacy had bogged down to a bloody stalemate. Thousands of men were dying on both sides—yet neither side could decisively gain the upper hand.

At this point, General Burnside suggested a plan for breaking the stalemate at Petersburg, Virginia. His idea involved tunneling into the Confederate defensive trench system and detonating a huge quantity of explosives. This would allow Union troops to enter the trenches and overrun the Confederate forces. General Ulysses S. Grant approved the plan, and Burnside was put in charge of implementing it.

So Far, So Good

Though the execution of the plan would prove disastrous, the plan itself was brilliantly conceived. A division of Pennsylvania infantry, most of them experienced coal miners, dug a five-hundred-foot tunnel under Confederate defensive lines. So far, so good. On July 30, 1864, the soldiers detonated a huge cache of explosives. The blast produced a hole 135 feet across (the crater is still visible today). More than three hundred Confederate soldiers were killed instantly by the explosion. The attack caught the forces of the South completely off guard, and they were too stunned to respond. A Union victory should have been certain.

But it was at precisely this point everything began to go wrong.

General James Ledlie, General Burnside's subordinate, sent a brigade of troops through the tunnel and into the crater. How had Burnside selected Ledlie to lead the operation? By casting lots! Ledlie was randomly chosen, even though he had already demonstrated his incompetence a month earlier in a disastrous charge at the Dimmock Line near Petersburg.

Because General Ledlie failed to brief his troops, they had no idea what they were supposed to do when they entered the crater. So they milled around at the bottom of the hole, waiting for orders. Those orders never came because, at the time the attack was launched, General Ledlie was drunk in his tent.

Moreover, General Burnside had failed to equip his soldiers with ladders. As a result, the troops had no way to climb up out of the crater and fan out into the trenches. As a result, the Confederate forces were able to regroup, gather around the rim of the crater, and fire down at the Union troops. It was like shooting fish in a barrel. The result was that fifty-three hundred Union soldiers were killed or wounded at the bottom of the crater.

What should have been a decisive victory for the North became a symbol of military ineptitude and the futility of war. The disaster at the crater ended the careers of both General Burnside and General Ledlie. The siege of Petersburg, Virginia, continued for another eight months at the cost of hundreds of additional lives.

Upon hearing the tragic outcome of General Burnside's plan, President Abraham Lincoln remarked, "Only Burnside could have snatched one more defeat from the jaws of victory."[1]

When I think of General Burnside's spectacular failure at Petersburg, I'm reminded that we believers often commit the same mistakes. We have a brilliant strategy, given to us by our Commander in Chief, Jesus Christ. We have all the resources we could want, provided for us by God the Father. We have begun well, and we are poised for victory. So far, so good.

But then our nerve, our faith, and our vision fail. We fail to claim the complete victory. Like General Burnside, we all too often have snatched defeat from the jaws of victory.

That's the situation in which Joshua and the nation of Israel now find themselves. Let's look at their story and see what lessons we can learn and apply to our own lives.

A Bloodthirsty God and Our Merciful God

In Joshua 10–12, we find the story of a bloody military campaign. Skeptics often cite this section of the Bible as proof that the God of the Old Testament was a cruel and bloodthirsty deity who violates the New Testament image of a God of love and grace. I want to answer that criticism and place this section of Joshua in a context showing why the God of the Old Testament and the God of the New Testament are one and the same.

If you take an honest look at the pagan Canaanite tribes, you see they practiced an idolatrous religion that was not only sexually immoral but unimaginably cruel and murderous. In the book of Leviticus, God told Moses, "You must not do as they do in Egypt, where you used to live, and you must not do as they do in the land of Canaan, where I am bringing you. Do not follow their practices" (18:3).

In the rest of the chapter, God lists some of the practices of the Canaanites, and they include various forms of incest, bestiality, and sexual perversion. Their practices also included the incomprehensible sacrifice of babies to their bloody god Molech: "Do not give any of your children to be sacrificed to Molech, for you must not profane the name of your God. I am the LORD" (Lev. 18:21).

Molech, also known as "Ba'al Moloch" or the "sacred bull," was a demonic Canaanite deity represented by an idol made of brass, shaped like a man with a bull's head and outstretched hands. Fires were stoked in the idol's belly or in a brazier beneath the hands. Unbelievable as it may seem, the priests of Molech would place living infants in the fires of the idol.[2]

Archaeologists have confirmed that the Canaanites and Amorites in the region did in fact practice the horrible kinds of perversions described in Leviticus. They actually sacrificed their own children in the fires. Researchers have also found funerary jars containing the remains of children who were buried alive, their bones bearing mute witness to their awful death agonies as they were offered to the horrific Canaanite deities.

The pagan societies of the land of Canaan had no regard for human life, not even the lives of their own children. So the heart of our merciful God was stirred and angered by these practices, and He told the Israelites through Moses:

> All these things were done by the people who lived in the land before you, and the land became defiled. And if you defile the land, it will vomit you out as it vomited out the nations that were before you.
>
> Everyone who does any of these detestable things—such persons must be cut off from their people. Keep my requirements and do not follow any of the detestable customs that were practiced before you came and do not defile yourselves with them. I am the LORD your God.
>
> (Lev. 18:27–30)

Is it any wonder, then, that God should send His people into the land of Canaan with instructions to exterminate these people and their grisly religious practices from the earth? Was God truly "bloodthirsty" in commanding the destruction of a culture that slaughtered children by fire and suffocation—

or was Israel's eradication of those cultures truly an act of mercy? Clearly, the reason God ordered the destruction of those people and their cities was to prevent Israel from being contaminated by their abominable practices.

The story of Canaan's conquest begins with the destruction of Jericho and Ai. In Joshua 10, we learn that King Adoni-Zedek of Jerusalem heard of the conquest of Jericho and Ai and the peace treaty between Gibeon and Israel. So he formed an alliance with the kings of four other Amorite cities, and together they made war against Gibeon. The Gibeonites then sent a message to Joshua: "Do not abandon your servants. Come up to us quickly and save us!" (Josh. 10:6).

So Joshua took his army to Gibeon. And as they went, the Lord said to Joshua, "Do not be afraid of them; I have given them into your hand" (Josh. 10:8). And Joshua took the five Amorite armies by surprise, and the Lord threw those armies into confusion. Not only did Israel defeat the Amorites and pursue them along the roads, but the Lord also sent hailstones down upon the Amorites, and more of them died from the hail than from the Israelites' swords.

And as the battle raged, Joshua called upon the Lord, praying that the sun would stand still over Gibeon and the moon would remain over the Valley of Aijalon. So the sun and the moon did not move in the sky until Israel had utterly vanquished its enemies.

Joshua proceeded to conquer the other pagan cities of the region—Makkedah, Libnah, Lachish, Eglon, Hebron, and Debir, until he had subdued the entire southern region of Canaan, from the hill country to the Negev desert. The Scripture text concludes, "All these kings and their lands Joshua conquered in one campaign because the LORD, the God of Israel, fought for Israel" (Josh. 10:42).

In Joshua 11 we read that Jabin, king of Hazor, formed an alliance with the kings of the north. These kings, the Scriptures tell us, "came out with all their troops and a large number of horses and chariots—a huge army, as numerous as the sand on the seashore. All these kings joined forces and made camp together at the Waters of Merom, to fight against Israel" (Josh. 11:4–5).

Again, the Lord told Joshua, "Do not be afraid of them, because by this time tomorrow I will hand all of them over to Israel, slain" (Josh. 11:6). So Joshua and his army surprised the enemy armies at the Waters of Merom. Again, the victorious army of Israel pursued the enemy along the roads and down the valleys and over the hills, leaving no survivors. The Scriptures tell us:

> As the LORD commanded his servant Moses, so Moses commanded Joshua, and Joshua did it; he left nothing undone of all that the LORD commanded Moses. . . . So Joshua took the entire land, just as the LORD had directed Moses, and he gave it as an inheritance to Israel according to their tribal divisions. Then the land had rest from war.
>
> (Josh. 11:15, 23)

Joshua 12 lists the kings and peoples whom Joshua and the army of Israel removed from the promised land—the Amorites, Canaanites, Hittites, Perizzites, Hivites, and Jebusites. It's a lengthy list! And you may wonder, *What does this long list of conquests and this bloody tale of war have to do with my life as a follower of Jesus Christ in the twenty-first century?*

Our Defeated Foe

One theme runs throughout these three chapters in the book of Joshua: *victory!* In the days of Joshua, armies fought with swords and shields, and victory took the form of vanquished kings and conquered cities. But God has a very different form of victory in mind for you and me. Victory, in the New Testament sense, does not involve warring against flesh and blood. Rather, our fight is against spiritual powers and authorities.

We sometimes make the mistake of thinking we are at war against human enemies, human institutions, and human political systems. Some organization wants to take God's name out of the Pledge of Allegiance or ban Bible clubs from public schools, and we think the people in that organization are the enemy.

While it's important to protect our First Amendment right to the free exercise of religion, we should not view any human individual or human institution as our enemy. We must never forget that "our struggle is not against flesh and blood, but against the rulers, against the authorities, against the powers of this dark world and against the spiritual forces of evil in the heavenly realms" (Eph. 6:12).

Our enemy is Satan and his rebellious angels. We are at war against spiritual strongholds of evil. And we easily forget that the victory has already been won! Satan has already been defeated! This does not mean that our enemy is not still dangerous. He is. He seeks to do as much harm to us as he can in the short time he has left before he is cast into the fires of eternal punishment.

But Jesus Christ has already defeated Satan. Though he still causes conflicts among believers, conflicts in families, strife in marriages, and spiritual blindness in the hearts of nonbelievers, he is a defeated foe. Satan may arouse hostility against our witness for Christ. He may send obstacles and discouragement our way. He may cause calamities and problems to distract us from our mission. But we must always remember that our heavenly Father has already won the victory over Satan.

Now the question that confronts us is this: Have we claimed the complete victory that is already ours in Jesus Christ? Have we claimed the complete victory so that we can finish this mopping-up operation against our defeated foe? Have we claimed the complete victory so we can experience victorious living in the here and now?

This is no time for a defeatist attitude. This is no time to let up. We must not surrender to discouragement or pessimism. Our enemy is on the run. There's no escape for him now. We have him where we want him. This is the time to claim the complete victory.

When we have done as the Lord has commanded us, leaving nothing undone, then, like Joshua, we can take the entire land the Lord has promised to us as our inheritance. Then, like Joshua and the Israelites, we will finally have rest from our long spiritual war.

How to Claim Victory

How do we claim the complete victory?

We do so by relentlessly focusing on our mission for Jesus Christ. We don't retreat. We don't let our guard down. We never forget that we are engaged in a spiritual struggle against spiritual strongholds. This is war and we conduct ourselves as soldiers.

The church of Jesus Christ was never meant to be a USO show where the troops are entertained. It was never meant to be a weekend pass for some R & R. The church is the headquarters for our campaign, the refueling station for an all-out offensive against Satan.

We are on the spiritual battlefront, engaged in a great struggle for the souls of men, women, and young people. We are combatants in a fight for the salvation of individuals and entire families. Our mission is to rescue the perishing, heal the wounded, and liberate the prisoners. Our objective is to break the chains of sin and addiction and to lead the way to victory, liberation, and a life of meaning and joy.

Yes, the victory has already been won on the cross at Calvary, but we must claim the complete victory for our own lives and the lives of those around us. God the Son emptied Himself of the glory He had in heaven. He was born of a virgin, lived for thirty-three years on earth, carried out His mission in Palestine, was crucified on a criminal's cross, was buried in a borrowed tomb, rose again on the third day, and ascended into heaven. Soon He is coming back. And friend in Christ, I want you to know He did not go through all of this so we, His children, could live defeated lives.

From Genesis to Revelation, God's message to us is that He has made it possible for us to experience the complete victory, both in this life and in the life to come. He has not given us a partial victory or an occasional victory, but total victory. And it is up to us to claim the victory and appropriate it for our lives, day by day by day.

There is a story told about a company of soldiers in the Korean War. Whether the story is true or not, I can't say. But either way, it's a great story that makes an important point.

Baker Company, a group of American soldiers, was cut off from the other American units and surrounded by enemy forces. The American military headquarters received no word from Baker Company for several hours. The corpsman at headquarters kept signaling by radio: "Baker Company, do you read? Baker Company, do you read?"

Finally, a reply was heard, faint and obscured by static. "This is Baker Company."

The corpsman asked, "What is your situation?"

Again, the reply came faintly. "The enemy is to the east of us . . . and to the north of us . . . and to the west of us . . . and to the south of us." There was a pause, then—"They can't get away from us now!"[3]

Sometimes, we feel surrounded and hemmed in on all sides by the enemy of our souls. At such times, we need to remember that we face a defeated enemy. He may have us surrounded, but all that means is he can't get away from us now. All we have to do is claim the victory that has already been won.

As you look around at the challenges you face, the problems that beset you, the seemingly impossible tasks before you, what is your response? Does it seem to you that it's time to panic? That it's time for despair? That it's time for surrender? Or do you see an opportunity for *victory*? Remember the words of the apostle Paul when he felt surrounded by spiritual opposition:

We are hard pressed on every side, but not crushed; perplexed, but not in despair; persecuted, but not abandoned; struck down, but not destroyed. . . . Therefore we do not lose heart. Though outwardly we are wasting away, yet inwardly we are being renewed day by day. For our light and momentary troubles are achieving for us an eternal glory that far outweighs them all. So we fix our eyes not on what is seen, but on what is unseen. For what is seen is temporary, but what is unseen is eternal.

(2 Cor. 4:8–9, 16–18)

Like Paul, you and I are hard-pressed on every side, but we know the victory has already been won. The opposition we face is temporary, but the victory we claim is eternal. We are surrounded by opposition, by unbelievers, by antagonists who hate the truth. But we rejoice, knowing they cannot get away from us now. Our mission is not to destroy them but to win them to Christ. And because God has already prepared their hearts for the gospel, witnessing to them is sort of like shooting fish in a barrel.

We do not retreat, because we are already conquerors. We have nothing to fear, and we have everything to celebrate.

War Is Confrontation

There are three important principles we learn from Joshua 10–12:

Principle 1: War begins with *confrontation.*
Principle 2: War is waged through *conflict.*
Principle 3: War concludes with *conquest.*

Let's look at each of these principles and apply them to the spiritual battles we face every day.

Principle 1: War Begins with Confrontation

Joshua and the army of Israel were surrounded by a united enemy. The tribes and kings that normally fought among themselves formed an alliance against Israel. The Canaanites, Amorites, and other tribes put aside their differences in order to confront the people of God. Joshua knew God had promised victory to Israel. He knew there had to be a confrontation.

Israel was surrounded by enemies—north, south, east, and west. The attitude of God's people was not "What is our escape route?" or "We're doomed!" or "Where's our white flag?" Though surrounded on all sides, their attitude was "Our enemy can't get away from us now!"

The historian Josephus estimates that the Israelites faced a force of 300,000 foot soldiers, 10,000 cavalry, and 20,000 chariots. For the nation of Israel, the promised land was hostile territory, to say the least. From a human perspective, the odds were overwhelmingly stacked against God's people. Any military strategist, applying commonsense principles to the situation, would have told Joshua that his situation was hopeless. But the confrontation Joshua faced was hopeless only if you took Jehovah out of the equation.

This same principle is true in all the battles you face. You may think the challenge God has given you is completely impossible. The confrontation you face may leave you overwhelmed and even paralyzed. Why? Because you are looking at this confrontation from a purely human perspective. You have left Jehovah out of the equation.

My friend, don't ever go into a battle without taking Jehovah with you.

Principle 2: War Is Waged Through Conflict

Do not be afraid of conflict with Satan. Take the battle to your enemy. Wage war against him, confident that the Lord goes before you into battle.

Joshua did not wait for the battle to come to him. He took the battle to the enemy. He knew the odds were stacked against him—but only from a human perspective. Yes, there were hundreds of thousands of soldiers and tens of thousands of cavalry and chariots arrayed against him. And as you study the passage closely, you realize Joshua felt fear. How do we know that? In just a moment, I'll show you.

We need to remember that Joshua was no supersaint. Just like you and me, he got rattled. His circumstances sometimes shook his faith. He had doubts.

Perhaps Joshua was thinking, *Are we truly in God's will? What if I have misunderstood His plan for Israel? What if there is a hidden sin in our midst and we suffer another defeat like the one at Ai? Will God be with us as He was at Jericho? Will He truly deliver us one more time?*

Doubts are not always reasonable or rational, but when doubts worm their way into our thinking, they *really* plague us.

God knows how our minds work. He understood the turmoil in Joshua's heart. So twice God said to Joshua, "Do not be afraid of them." And each time, God followed that word of assurance with a promise of victory:

> Do not be afraid of them; I have given them into your hand.
>
> (Josh. 10:8)
>
> Do not be afraid of them, because by this time tomorrow I will hand all of them over to Israel, slain.
>
> (Josh. 11:6)

Here's an important principle of Scripture study. The Lord never wastes His words. God does not tell people, "Do not be afraid," unless those people are afraid! So, whenever you read that God or one of His angelic messengers said to someone, "Do not be afraid," you can be sure this person was experiencing fear.

When the Lord appeared to Abram (later called Abraham) to make a covenant with him, His opening words were "Do not be afraid" (Gen. 15:1). When the Lord appeared to Abraham's son Isaac, He said again, "Do not be afraid" (Gen. 26:24). When Jacob was afraid to go down to Egypt, God spoke to him and said, "Do not be afraid" (Gen. 46:3). When Moses faced war with the Amorites, God encouraged Moses, saying, "Do not be afraid" (Num. 21:34). When God sent the prophet Elijah to confront an idolatrous king, God gave the prophet these reassuring words: "Do not be afraid" (2 Kings 1:15).

When the angel of the Lord appeared to Mary, the mother of Jesus the Messiah, she was troubled and perhaps even terrified at the angel's sudden appearance. So the angel said to her, "Do not be afraid, Mary, you have found favor with God" (Luke 1:30). Later, the angel appeared to shepherds in the fields and announced to them the birth of the Savior; as the shepherds trembled in terror, the angel said, "Do not be afraid" (Luke 2:10).

At least two times in the life of the apostle Paul, God told him, "Do not be afraid." The first time was when Paul was preaching in the synagogues of Corinth and facing intense opposition. The Lord Himself told Paul, "Do not be afraid; keep on speaking, do not be silent" (Acts 18:9). Years later, when Paul was a prisoner aboard a ship in danger of breaking apart in a raging storm, God sent an angel with a message: "Do not be afraid, Paul. . . . God has graciously given you the lives of all who sail with you" (Acts 27:24).

We tend to think that the heroes of the Bible never knew the meaning of fear. That is simply not true! There were times when their knees knocked, their hands shook, and they became so tongue-tied they could hardly speak. So the next time you feel afraid, remember that you are in good company. The great heroes of the Bible are at your side, trembling and stammering right along with you!

But also remember that the Lord Himself is also at your side—and His word to you is "Don't be afraid. The victory is already yours."

What fear holds you back from accepting God's challenge for your life? You may say, "I don't feel qualified to share Christ with other people." That's all right. I don't feel qualified either. In fact, it's a good sign if you don't feel qualified. That means the next time you share your faith with someone else, you will be relying on God's strength instead of your own. So if you don't feel qualified, rejoice! You're exactly the kind of person God uses.

This is very important: if you allow fear to drive you into retreat and surrender, and if you shrink back from claiming your workplace, your campus, or your neighborhood for Christ, you will be doing nothing less than snatching defeat from the jaws of victory. You may try to rationalize your retreat and defeat by saying, "I can't be a witness. I'm only one person. My plate is full right now. I'll just be a private Christian, and I'll go to church, read the Scripture, have my quiet time with the Lord, and that will be enough."

But let me tell you something. If you retreat from the battle for the lost souls of the men, women, and children around you, it will not be long before the enemy has defeated you in all of those other areas. Your prayer life will wither up and blow away. Your church attendance will become a meaningless routine. Your fellowship with other believers will become a series of shallow social events. And you will wonder why you don't seem to connect with God anymore.

That is why it is so important to claim the complete victory, to stay on the offensive for Christ, to remain focused on our mission for Christ, to maintain our burning passion for Christ. In order to claim the complete victory, we must take the battle to the enemy, not wait for the battle to come to us. We must continually seek to expand God's kingdom. We must constantly seek to rescue lost souls from the oppressive grip of our foe.

If you will stay on the offensive and take the battle to the enemy and claim the complete victory, then you will have victory in all areas of your life. Your prayer life will be vibrant. Your worship will be rich and meaningful. Your fellowship will be deep and dynamic. And every day of your walk with Christ will be an exciting new adventure.

Principle 3: War Concludes with Conquest

Joshua 11 says conclusively: "So Joshua took the entire land, just as the LORD had directed Moses, and he gave it as an inheritance to Israel according to their tribal divisions. Then the land had rest from war" (Josh. 11:23).

When we have achieved the conquest, when we have the victory, we can finally have rest from war. The conquest does not happen easily or overnight. Conquest requires perseverance, dedication, and patience.

I am reminded of a story from the early history of colonial

Australia. The first Australian-born explorer was Hamilton Hume (1797–1873). In late 1824, Hume led an expedition to map the land and rivers of the region known as New South Wales. His goal was to move southeast through the interior until the expedition reached the southern coast of Australia.

Along the way, Hume and his men experienced a crisis. They came face-to-face with a mountain range that seemed to block their way. The men were exhausted and utterly discouraged. They begged Hume to give up, turn back, and go home.

Hume pointed to the high mountain ahead and said, "If we attain that summit, I know that we will see the ocean. We will have found what we are looking for, and we can return home and tell others of our success."

So Hume and his men climbed the mountain. When they reached the summit, they looked out to where Hume had said the ocean would be. There was no ocean. There was nothing but miles and miles of ridges and gullies and forests. Their goal was nowhere in sight.

On the map they were drawing, they marked the location of the mountain upon which they stood and named it "Mount Disappointment." Then they swallowed their own bitter disappointment, started down the other side of the ridge, and persevered in their journey—until they finally reached the shore at Corio Bay.

The Hume expedition proved that the interior of Australia was habitable and filled with well-watered grazing land. Soon, settlers streamed into the interior of the continent. Today, the formidable mountain range that made some of Hume's men want to turn back is known as the Hume Range, and millions of people now drive the Hume Highway from Sydney to Melbourne.[4]

Life is filled with Mount Disappointments. You have the choice to climb your mountains of disappointment by the power of Jehovah—or you can give up.

Whatever your Mount Disappointment may be, God is calling you to conquer it. He is calling you to endure disappointment and persevere over those ridges, to patiently traverse those gullies until you reach your victorious destination.

Joshua knew God had already promised the land to him and his people. He knew God had already given them the victory. All he had to do in order to claim the complete victory was to stay on the offensive, to refuse to surrender, to remain focused on his calling until the conquest was complete and the land had rest from war.

And if I know anything at all about God and His will for our lives, I know this: He wants the same thing for you and for me. He wants us to settle for nothing less than total victory, to pray for nothing less than total victory, to sacrifice for nothing less than total victory.

When Satan comes after you, do not be afraid. Stand your ground, because your enemy is already defeated. Take the battle to your foe, and God will give you the complete victory.

9

You Want Me to Trust in the Cosmic Real Estate Developer?

Joshua 13–17

In 1993, I was invited to speak at a breakfast hosted by the Atlanta chapter of the Urban Land Institute, an organization made up largely of real estate professionals. They asked me to give a brief talk, then lead in prayer. As I took the podium and gazed out over the crowd, I could see a look on many faces that seemed to ask, "Who is this guy?"

So I began by saying, "My name is Michael Youssef, and I work for the largest Real Estate Developer in the whole universe. I talk to Him every day about helping you guys with your real estate deals, and I ask Him to give you a part of His action." After I said those words, their looks gave way to laughter.

Then I led a prayer.

Now, the vast majority of the people in that room got the

point I was making. They knew I was talking about the heavenly Real Estate Developer, and that I wanted each person in that room to become a partner with God and a stakeholder in His kingdom.

But two or three individuals missed the point. They came up to me later, handed me their business cards, and said, "If we can do business with your boss, please have him call me at this number." They knew I was from the Middle East, and they assumed I had connections with an Arab trillionaire!

Now, I wasn't trying to fool anybody. What I said was the absolute, literal truth! My Boss is the largest Real Estate Developer in the entire universe, bar none. And He chooses to give each of us a territory in which to operate.

And as you come to the next section of Joshua, you will discover that chapters 13–17 are all about real estate. So it occurred to me that the theme of these chapters had to be, *You want me to do* what? *You want me to trust in the cosmic Real Estate Developer?*

Now that the people of Israel have crossed over the river of impossibility, shouted down the walls of Jericho, cleansed the land of the abhorrent practices of the Canaanites, and claimed the complete victory God has given them, there is still one thing left for them to do. They must divide the land of promise among the tribes of Israel.

This is the land the Lord promised to Abraham four centuries earlier. God had commanded them not only to conquer the land, but also to distribute the land among God's people. In Joshua 13–17, we have a detailed explanation of how the land was to be divided. We won't dwell on the details, but we can draw some lessons of vital importance from this portion of God's Word.

God Is Not Arbitrary

As Joshua 13 opens, we see that a great deal of time has passed. Joshua is an old man. Now the Lord speaks to him about the apportioning of the land. So Joshua divides the promised land among the tribes of Israel, and every tribe except the Levites receives a tract of real estate.

Here is the lesson of vital importance we find in this passage—God gives us our territory based on our measure of faith. God gives us our blessings and our opportunities. The Scriptures tell us, "Every good and perfect gift is from above, coming down from the Father of the heavenly lights" (James 1:17). "When [Jesus] ascended on high, he . . . gave gifts to men" (Eph. 4:8). God wants His children to discover their gifts, use their gifts, invest their gifts, and put their gifts to work for Him.

You may ask, "How does God divide territories—opportunities and blessings—among His children today? How do I know what my territory is?" Answer: God does not divide His territories on an arbitrary basis. He distributes them on the basis of each believer's faithfulness to God.

We see this principle clearly in the example of the tribe of Reuben. According to ancient Hebrew custom, the firstborn is entitled to a double portion of the inheritance (see Deut. 21:15-17). But the tribe of Reuben, the firstborn of Israel, did not get a double portion. In fact, the Reubenites received a smaller and less desirable portion of the land. Why?

Reuben, the ancestor of the Reubenite tribe, committed sexual sin with the handmaid of Jacob's wife, Rachel (see Gen. 35:22). Years later, as Jacob lay dying, he told his eldest son, "Reuben, you are my firstborn. . . . Turbulent as the waters, you will no longer excel, for you went up onto your father's bed, onto my couch and defiled it" (Gen. 49:3-4).

According to human wisdom and tradition, an extra portion of an inheritance should be allocated to the first in line simply because of birth order. But God does not follow human traditions. He looks upon the heart. He judges our works. So the tribe of Reuben, the firstborn, received a smaller portion because of Reuben's unfaithfulness.

God allocated Reuben's territory in this way to illustrate a spiritual principle for our lives: our faithfulness (or lack of it) determines the territory we will receive. The sincerity of our hearts and the quality of our way of life are the determining factors in the levels of responsibility and blessing God gives to us.

Now, the Levites—the tribe of Levi—received no land whatsoever. Why? Because they were the priests and were called to minister to all of Israel, regardless of tribal boundaries and borders. The book of Joshua explains it this way: "But to the tribe of Levi, Moses had given no inheritance; the LORD, the God of Israel, is their inheritance, as he promised them" (Josh. 13:33).

So the territories of the Levites were spiritual in nature. They received no real estate because their *true* estate was God Himself.

Now, you might ask, "What was God up to? His decisions seem unfair. He gave the Reubenites a smaller portion because their ancestor sinned long before they themselves were born. Why should they be penalized for the sin of Reuben?

"And what about the Levites? The Scriptures say they received no inheritance because God was their inheritance—but how did they feel as the promised land was divided and everybody got a share except them? Did they really think that was fair?"

You might say, as some skeptics have said, "God's actions seem arbitrary and unjust. Didn't God understand that a lop-sided distribution of the land would cause only tension, bitterness, and envy among His people?"

The answer: God is not unjust. When His actions are different from what we expect or approve of, it's because His ways are not our ways, and His understanding is so much greater and deeper than ours. God sees the beginning and the end together. We don't. He sees the past, present, and future as one. We don't. He knows the secrets of every human heart, and the motives and intentions of every human mind. We don't.

God knows the future better than we know our own pasts. He gives us territories and opportunities based on our measure of faith, based on His foreknowledge. He sets our borders and boundaries on the basis of His perfect knowledge, not on our imperfect and selfish desires. Our understanding of God's actions and decisions is imperfect because we view reality from a subjective point of view—but God's viewpoint is perfect because it is not only objective, but omniscient as well.

Three Money Managers

You might ask, "How can I do more for God? How can I be more for God?" Jesus gives us the answer to that question in Matthew 25:14–30. There He tells the story of a boss and three money managers.

The boss gives each of the three money managers a quantity of money, a different sum for each one. To put it in today's terms, the boss gave one of them $5,000. He gave the next in line $2,000. And he gave the last in line $1,000. Was this boss being unfair? No. He knew the heart of each of these money managers. He already knew in advance how each one would carry out his responsibility.

The man who was entrusted with $5,000 invested his money and brought back a return of $5,000 more. He doubled his investment. And the man who was entrusted with $2,000 invested his money and brought back a return of $2,000 more.

When the boss received an accounting from each of these individuals, he commended both of them equally. He didn't expect the man with $2,000 to go out and triple or quadruple his investment. The man with $2,000 had doubled his investment, just as the man with $5,000.

The boss commended both of these money managers with exactly the same words: "Well done, good and faithful servant! You have been faithful with a few things; I will put you in charge of many things. Come and share your master's happiness!" (Matt. 25:21, 23). He said the same words to both men because he was a just and fair boss, just as the God he symbolizes is just and fair.

But what about the money manager who received only $1,000 to invest? When he was given the smallest quantity of money, he went out and held a pity party. Those words aren't in the Bible, but that's exactly what he did. He said to himself, "Poor me! The boss didn't give me as much as he gave those other guys! What am I supposed to do with one lousy grand to invest? That's chicken feed! The boss doesn't trust me! I've been slighted! I'm insulted! This is so unfair!"

Don't you hate it when people hold pity parties? Instead of going out and doing something with what they've been given, they sit and whine about what they don't have. After all, the boss had given him *something* to work with. A thousand bucks might be "chump change" to Bill Gates or Warren Buffett, but this man's boss had given him a real opportunity to prove what he could do—and he blew it.

The man took his $1,000, dug a hole in the backyard, and buried it. He didn't invest it. He didn't double it. He didn't do anything with it. He foolishly stuck it in the ground and covered it with dirt.

Now, I ask you: would this man have responded any differently if he had been given $2,000 or $5,000? No. This man's boss had given him the smallest quantity of money to manage because he knew what kind of man he was. He knew this money manager could not be trusted with a larger sum. He knew this man would not be faithful in managing small blessings, small opportunities, or small territories.

If we are not faithful with the small things, how can we be trusted with the big things? But the good servant, who is faithful in a few things, will be placed in charge of many things. As Jesus said, the good servant will share in the joy of his Master and Lord, both in this life and in the life to come.

When God gives you a small blessing, a small opportunity to minister, a small territory in which to work, He is watching to see how you handle it. All of your future blessings, opportunities, and territories depend on how you handle the challenges He gives you today.

The Example of Caleb

In Joshua 14, we see that Joshua's longtime comrade, Caleb, was singled out for a special gift; the greatest and most desirable territory: "Joshua blessed Caleb son of Jephunneh and gave him Hebron as his inheritance" (Josh. 14:13). As we shall soon see, Caleb is a role model and a challenge to us all. We should ask ourselves, *Why was Caleb singled out and honored by God? Why did he receive a larger portion than the rest? What can we learn and apply to our own lives from the example of Caleb?*

To answer this question, we need to understand who Caleb was and what he did. In Numbers 13, when the Israelites were in the wilderness, Moses sent out a committee of twelve spies to explore the promised land. Moses approached this mission in a democratic fashion, asking each of the twelve tribes to select one representative to go into the promised land.

The twelve men went in and spied out the land. They examined the agricultural and economic possibilities of the land. They looked at the Canaanites' cities, the populations, the infrastructures, and the defenses. Then they returned to Moses and the Israelite tribes and presented two separate reports—a majority report and a minority report.

When the vote was taken among them, the vote was ten to two. Ten of the twelve spies said, in effect, "The land is full of giants. Those guys are huge! They will eat our lunch! And then they will eat *us* for lunch! We can't win against these Canaanites. We're no match for them. We would have been better off if we had died in the wilderness." The majority report was nothing but doom and gloom.

But the remaining two spies offered a very different perspective. "The majority report is nonsense," they said. "We have nothing to be afraid of! So what if the Canaanites all look like Arnold Schwarzenegger? They are like gnats next to our God! The Lord has promised to go with us. With God on our side, no enemy can stand against us! Let's go!"

The majority was wrong. The minority was right. By now,

if you didn't already know, you have probably figured out the identity of the two courageous and faithful spies. Their names were Joshua and Caleb.

These two men were later singled out for their great faithfulness to God. Joshua became a successor to Moses and the leader of the nation of Israel during the crisis years of the conquest of the promised land. And after the land was conquered, Caleb was singled out for honor and reward when the real estate of the promised land was divided and distributed.

A Man of Optimistic Faith

You don't need a seminary degree to understand what the example of Caleb is saying to us: God loves faith. God loves optimism that trusts in His promises. He loves to see His people daring to take risks for the sake of His kingdom. God is honored and happy to see us operating in childlike trust in Him.

Caleb was a man of optimistic faith. He reminds me of the farmer who was going through tough times, but who trusted in the Lord to provide for his needs. The farmer went to see his banker one day, saying, "I've got good news and bad news. Let me start with the bad news. Because of the current drought and economic conditions, I won't be able to make any payments on my mortgage this year, neither the principle nor the interest."

The banker frowned. "Oh, that's bad news."

"There's more," the farmer said. "I also won't be able to make any payments on the loan you gave me for my farm machinery."

The banker looked even more troubled. "Oh, that's *very* bad news."

"One more thing," the farmer said. "I also have a loan with your bank for my seed and fertilizer."

"Oh, no," the banker said. "Don't tell me—"

"That's right," the farmer said. "I can't make those payments either."

"That's terrible news," the banker said. "But you said you also have some good news."

"I certainly do," the farmer said. "The good news is that I'm going to continue doing business with you."

Now *that's* an optimist! That's the kind of man Caleb was. Where ten other men saw giants, Caleb saw gnats. Where ten other men saw obstacles, Caleb saw opportunities. Where ten other men saw fear and terror, Caleb saw faith and power. Where ten other men saw impossibility, Caleb saw the promise of God. Where ten other men saw nothing but defeat, Caleb saw God's certain victory. Where ten other men saw nothing but a bleak future, Caleb saw the God who holds the future. Where ten other men saw only hopelessness, Caleb beheld the God of all hope.

So here in Joshua 14, we see that Caleb went to Joshua and said,

I was forty years old when Moses the servant of the LORD sent me from Kadesh Barnea to explore the land. And I brought him back a report according to my convictions, but my brothers who went up with me made the hearts of the people melt with fear. I, however, followed the LORD my God wholeheartedly. So on that day Moses swore to me, "The land on which your feet have walked will be your inheritance and that of your children forever, because you have followed the LORD my God wholeheartedly."

Now then, just as the LORD promised, he has kept me alive for forty-five years since the time he said this to Moses, while

Israel moved about in the desert. So here I am today, eighty-five years old! I am still as strong today as the day Moses sent me out; I'm just as vigorous to go out to battle now as I was then. Now give me this hill country that the LORD promised me that day. You yourself heard then that the Anakites were there and their cities were large and fortified, but, the LORD helping me, I will drive them out just as he said.

(Josh. 14:7–12)

So Joshua, under the guidance of the Lord, blessed Caleb and gave him the region of Hebron as his inheritance. As I read that story, I thought, *Wow! Caleb was eighty-five years old, and he was ready to pick up his sword and go right back into the fray!* And I tell you, I wanted to pump iron when I read those words. I figured if Caleb could do that at age eighty-five, I can do it too!

Caleb is a challenge to all of us who might be tempted to retire from God's work. Caleb had earned the right to go out and sit by the pool or play golf all day. But that's not the kind of man he was. He wasn't ready to retire to Sunset Acres. If there was still a fight to be fought anyplace in the promised land, Caleb intended to lead the charge.

Give Us More Calebs

A few years ago I went to California's Silicon Valley, south of San Francisco, to speak to a group of largely tech-sector businesspeople. One of the people there was a longtime friend of mine who had moved to California from Atlanta. He took me aside and said, "One of the things you need to know about this crowd is that most of them have a certain attitude toward their careers. As they see it, if you don't become financially independent so that you can retire by age forty-five, they look down on you as a failure."

I said, "Are you kidding me? What do they do with their time?"

"Well," my friend said, "they play a lot of golf and they manage their own investments."

I must tell you, I was totally flabbergasted by that mind-set. Why would anyone want to reach the end of a career so early in life? How does anyone derive a meaningful life from knocking a little white ball from hole to hole and shuffling stocks and bonds on a computer screen? If I had to spend every day of my life on a golf course, I'd feel that I had been put out to pasture!

May God give us more Calebs! May God give us more men and women who never give up on the promises of God, who never retire from the work of God, who never waver from their faith in God. May God give us more people of faith and optimism and an eager desire to spend their last breath in service to God.

There's a story about a shoe manufacturing company that sent a sales representative to open a new office in a foreign country. The man went to the foreign country, then returned, despondent, with a discouraging report. "It's hopeless," the man said. "We can't do any business in that country. No one wears shoes there."

The company decided to send another sales representative to see if the first man was right. Within a week, the second sales rep—who was a man much like Caleb—sent a telegram to the home office that read, "Send all the shoes you can! The market here is limitless! Everybody here needs shoes!"

Both of these sales reps saw exactly the same conditions, but the reports they sent back were like night and day. The reason: The first sales rep was a pessimist and the second sales rep was an optimist. The second man had faith like Caleb.

Even at age eighty-five, Caleb wasn't ready to rest on his blessed assurance and collect his pension. No, he was ready for one more fight! He was ready to tangle with giants! He was ready to take on the Anakites! He couldn't wait to take that hill for God!

If you want to increase your territory, if you want to be blessed by God, if you want to enlarge your opportunities for witnessing, serving, and expanding the kingdom of God, then remember the words of Jesus: "Well done, good and faithful servant! You have been faithful with a few things; I will put you in charge of many things. Come and share your master's happiness!" (Matt. 25:21). So be faithful with the little things, and don't be surprised when He entrusts you with something *big*.

Through the Eyes of Faith

I remember when The Church of The Apostles began. We had twenty-eight people meeting in a function room at the Waverly Hotel. People looked at the small beginnings of our church, and they said of me, "That poor Egyptian! He's lost his mind. He's talking about building a three-thousand-seat sanctuary someday. He's delusional!"

I had a friend in those days who was not a believer, but I had the joy and privilege of leading him to the Lord. He owned a great amount of real estate, and he became a great supporter of The Church of The Apostles. He once gave his testimony in church before he passed away, and he said, "I owe Michael Youssef an apology. I used to think, 'Poor Michael, he's a nice enough fellow, but he is crazy. He has lost his sanity.' But now

I understand. Now I see what Michael saw through the eyes of faith."

Through the eyes of faith, you are able to see things that other people do not see, things that do not exist—but that will exist one day. Through the eyes of faith, you learn to not despise small beginnings. You learn that if you are faithful with little things, God will trust you with bigger things.

Caleb could have asked Joshua for a golf course, a place where he could be quietly put out to pasture. Instead, Caleb asked Joshua for one more hill to climb, one more city to conquer. He said, in effect, "Give me the assignment that no one else will take. Give me the mountain that no one else will climb. Hand me my sword. God has one more job for me to do."

There are all kinds of Calebs in this world—people who could easily sit back and remain safe, yet they choose to accept a tough assignment. They choose to climb that mountain no one else will climb. They risk everything and ask for nothing in return.

One such "Caleb" was sixteen-year-old Blair Holt. Blair loved Air Jordan shoes, rap music, and hanging out with his friends. He enjoyed recording his own music at a local studio and giving out CDs to his friends at school. His rap name was Bizzy B. Most days, he would put in a couple of hours after school, working at a neighborhood grocery store owned by his grandparents—though he was hoping to get a job soon at the local Subway sandwich shop.

Blair Holt was a good student and his teachers at Julian High School loved having him in their classrooms. He was a happy, bighearted kid growing up in a tough neighborhood on the south side of Chicago. His dad was a police officer and his mother a firefighter. Every school day, his mother would drop him off at school. Her parting words as he got out of the car were always, "Do good, Blair."

After school, Blair would board a Chicago Transit Authority bus for a forty-minute ride to his grandparents' store. One day in May 2007, Blair was seated on the bus when an angry, tough-looking teenager boarded at 103rd and Halsted streets in the Roseland section. The bus pulled away from the curb and continued down 103rd. It was about 3:20 in the afternoon.

Standing in the aisle, the tough-looking teen pulled a .40-caliber semiautomatic handgun from his coat. He pointed the gun at someone in the middle of the bus and began shooting.

Blair Holt was not the target. He was not even in the line of fire. He could easily have ducked behind the seat and protected himself from harm. But Blair saw a girl from his school, Tiara Reed, sitting right in the area where the young gunman was firing. Blair jumped from his seat, threw himself on the girl, and shielded her with his body.

By the time the gunman was through shooting, Blair and four other innocent bystanders had been wounded. The bus pulled over, and the gunman got away. So did the teenage boy who was the young gunman's target—he had somehow escaped getting hit by the hail of bullets.

Ambulances and police arrived quickly in response to cell-phone calls to 911. Blair was rushed to the hospital, shot in the chest but conscious. On the way to the hospital, Blair asked paramedics to tell his mom and dad that he loved them. Doctors tried to save Blair, but he died that night at 9:03. It was the Thursday night before Mother's Day weekend, and Blair's mother spent that weekend making funeral arrangements for her only child.

The day before Mother's Day, Tiara Reed visited Blair's mother, Annette Holt, and told her that Blair had saved her life. The gunshot that took his life had been aimed at her. "Blair is a hero to me," Tiara said.

"If a parent went shopping to find the right child," Annette Holt later said, "Blair would be it. I'm so proud of my baby. To hear that my son was a hero is tremendous. I would do anything to get him back, though. I wish it was me. I wish it was me."[1]

The last morning of Blair Holt's life, his mother had said to him what she always said when she dropped him off at school. "Do good, Blair," she said.

"I will," he replied. And he did.

Someone once said, "You can take the measure of a man by the size of the challenges he undertakes." Though he was just sixteen years old, Blair Holt was a Caleb-sized man. He could have chosen safety; instead, he chose risk and self-sacrifice. He chose a challenge. He chose to do good.

What about you? What about me? We are confronted by great challenges. The blessings of heaven are going unclaimed because God's people have not been faithful with the little they have been given.

So the question that the cosmic Real Estate Developer has for you and me is this: Will you say, "Lord, give me a nice quiet golf course in the valley"? Will you say, "Give me safety and security and a life without challenges"?

Or will you say, "Lord, give me that mountain to climb, give me that city to conquer, give me that battle to fight"? Even in his old age, Caleb was ready for action, reporting for duty.

How about you?

10

You Want Me to Claim My Inheritance?

Question: What is the easiest thing in the world to do?

Answer: To quit!

Quitting takes no effort, no time, and no thought. And quitting is cheap! It won't cost you a dime. All you have to do is simply stop what you're doing.

Perseverance is hard; quitting is easy. Endurance is hard; quitting is easy. Courage is hard; quitting is easy. The easiest thing in the world to do is to quit.

Of course, there's a catch. If everybody does what comes easy, nothing will ever get accomplished. There'd be no cities, no highways, no railroads if everybody quit when things got hard. No books would ever be written, no symphonies would ever be performed, and no motion pictures would ever be shown if everybody quit when things got hard.

Israel would never have been delivered from bondage in

Egypt if Moses had quit when things got hard. And Israel never would have possessed the promised land if Joshua had quit when things got hard. We would still be lost in our sins if Jesus had quit when things got hard. And the fledgling church would never have expanded beyond the city limits of Jerusalem if Peter and Paul and the other apostles had quit when things got hard.

Now, as we come to Joshua 18, we encounter a disturbing incident. We see that God's people are on the verge of quitting. After all that God has brought them through, after all they have accomplished through faith in Him, they are about to take the easy way out.

They are about to quit.

"How Long Will You Wait?"

Let's look at the passage and we will see that Joshua is on the brink of absolute frustration and exasperation with his people—and with good reason:

> The whole assembly of the Israelites gathered at Shiloh and set up the Tent of Meeting there. The country was brought under their control, but there were still seven Israelite tribes who had not yet received their inheritance. So Joshua said to the Israelites: "How long will you wait before you begin to take possession of the land that the LORD, the God of your fathers, has given you? Appoint three men from each tribe. I will send them out to make a survey of the land and to write a description of it, according to the inheritance of each. Then they will return to me."
>
> (Josh. 18:1-4)

Joshua's exasperation with the people is obvious in the phrase "How long will you wait . . . ?" He is saying, in effect, "What's wrong with you people? What's taking you so long? What are you waiting for? The Lord has given you this land as an inheritance! Why haven't you claimed it? Why haven't you settled it? Why haven't you developed it?"

God has been powerfully, supernaturally guiding the people of Israel. He has led them across the river of impossibility. He has enabled them to demolish the impenetrable walls of Jericho with a shout. He has given them the complete victory, even though their enemies had superior weapons, armor, and fortifications—and vastly greater numbers. The people of Israel have received miracle after miracle from the hand of God.

The hard work has been done. The enemies have been vanquished, the wars have been won, and now the land is at rest. All that remains is for the tribes of Israel to divide the land among themselves. And that is what Joshua was doing in the previous chapter. Now comes the easy part. The people simply have to pull up in their U-Haul Rent-a-Camel, unload their worldly goods, and take possession of the real estate God has given them.

What could be easier?

Yet they have not done so. They have quit before the job was finished. It appears that seven of the tribes have gotten so used to a nomadic lifestyle—a life of wandering the hills and deserts without ever putting down roots—that they are squandering the inheritance God has given them.

The Lord told Israel, in effect, "Here is your estate. Here are the keys to the mansion. The pool, the tennis courts, and all the other amenities are yours. Those acres over there are your vineyards. And the trees on those hills are your orchards. All of this is yours to enjoy and to pass on to your children and your children's children."

And the seven tribes have replied, in effect, "Thanks, but no thanks. We've gotten kind of used to driving around the countryside in this beat-up old Volkswagen bus. Sure, it's cramped and uncomfortable, and the tires are bald and the transmission is shot, but to us, it's home. What would we want with the mansion?"

The inheritance is theirs. The deed has already been recorded in their name. All they have to do is claim it—yet they stubbornly settle for second best.

No Waves of Conversions

The Israelites have come so far, and they have endured so much. They have seen God carry them through one crisis after another. It is as if they have run a marathon—a footrace of 26 miles, 385 yards—and they have decided to call it quits after 26 miles, 384 yards, just three feet short of the finish line. Why would anyone come so far and endure so much only to quit when the prize is just inches from their grasp?

Before we criticize these Israelites too harshly, we should recognize that these "quitters" are actually a symbolic picture of so many of us as professing Christians. Various surveys have shown that there are around forty million people in America who call themselves "evangelicals."[1] Now, the word *evangelical* comes from the Latin word *evangelium*, which means "good news." So an evangelical *should* be a person who believes in spreading the good news of faith in Jesus Christ.

If there truly are forty million evangelicals in America, then there should be forty million evangelists witnessing and sharing Christ on a daily basis in their neighborhoods, offices, and schools. There should be waves of conversions sweeping the nation as forty million evangelists tell everyone they know how to have a personal relationship with Jesus Christ.

Obviously, this is not happening. Instead, we have a church that is anemic and ineffective. There are no waves of conversions sweeping the country. Why is that? Why are so many professing Christians today living mediocre lives and having no impact on the world around them? Why does the church have so little impact on our society?

It's because we, like the seven tribes of Israel, have refused to claim our inheritance. We have decided that we would rather live in sin and disobedience to the Word of God than truly become the people God wants us to be. Oh, we will still claim to be His children. We will go to church on Sundays. And when the pollsters come around, we will tell them, "Yes, we are evangelicals. We are professing Christians."

But we will not share the good news with anyone around us. In fact, we will remain so quiet and secretive about our Christian faith that our neighbors, our colleagues at work, and our fellow students will not even have a clue that we are followers of Jesus Christ.

So you see, we are just like those Israelites. We have come so far in our Christian life. We have experienced the miracle of salvation and liberation from guilt and sin. God has brought us over many rivers of impossibility. He has enabled us to conquer addictions, sinful habits, troubled relationships, health problems, depression, and many other crises in our lives. He has enabled us to run the long, arduous marathon of this life.

Yet, with the finish line within easy reach, we have quit.

We have chosen silence. We are too busy, or too selfish, or simply too embarrassed to talk about our faith in Christ.

Let me tell you about a man who goes out of his way to share Christ with others. In fact, I already introduced this man to you in chapter 1. His name is Art Fowler, and I told you how he flew from Colorado to Florida just so he could visit football player Mercury Morris in prison and share the good news of Jesus Christ with him. Let me tell you of another way that Art Fowler shares Jesus Christ with other people.

"One thing I've done many times," he says, "is to get behind a police car and pull an officer over. I flick my lights at him and sometimes honk the horn. He'll pull over, and I'll stop my car behind his. Usually the officer will wait for me to get out of my car and approach him. Obviously, he doesn't know who I am or what I want, so he's cautious. When I come up to the window, I know that the officer has one hand on his gun, which is one reason I don't recommend this kind of witnessing to everybody.

"Usually, I'll have my business card in my hand and I'll give it to the officer and say something like, 'Hey, I know you guys have a tough job, and I just wanted to say thanks for being there, protecting the public. I want you to know I support you guys. I'm sure there are a lot of problems and struggles in your line of work. I'm a counselor, and a pretty good listener, and if you ever need someone to talk to, just call me at the number on the card, anytime, no charge.'

"Well, that's usually all I need to say to get the conversation started. Before long, the officer and I are talking about what's going on in his life, and I always find a way to let him know that Jesus loves him. Sometimes we just talk by the side of the road and other times I've ridden along with them on patrol. I've seen at least a couple hundred officers come to know Christ in this way. I've never had an officer get upset with me. They always seem to appreciate the words of support and encouragement."[2]

The next time you are tempted to think, *I don't have time to share Christ with my neighbor,* or, *What will this person think of me if I tell him about Jesus?* or, *I don't want anyone to think I am a religious fanatic,* I want you to remember Art Fowler. I want you to remember a man who pulls policemen over by the side of the road to talk to them about Jesus Christ. Then ask yourself this question: *What does God want me to do in this situation? Who does the Lord want me to talk to right now?*

We have kept the good news of Jesus Christ to ourselves. We have treated the gospel as if it is our little secret. We have neglected the blessing that comes when we share our faith and lead others to Christ. We have refused to rescue others from the oppression of the enemy and bring them into the Kingdom of Light.

One of the greatest thrills of being a believer, one of the most exhilarating experiences of knowing Christ, is the experience of leading another person to Christ. When you have a part in sharing that good news with another human soul, and when that person responds to your message and asks Jesus to become their Lord and Savior, you feel a tingle down your spine, a flutter in your chest, and tears of joy springing in your eyes. There is nothing in the world that compares with such joy.

Have you ever felt it? Have you ever shared Christ with another person? Have you ever experienced the thrill of watching a soul pass from death to eternal life? If not, why not?

God has spread a spiritual feast of joy before you! Why are you living on the spiritual equivalent of food stamps?

God has given you the deed to the palace. Why are you settling for the spiritual ghetto?

God has given you millions of megawatts of spiritual power—more than enough to claim your workplace, your school, or your neighborhood for Him. Why are you choosing to live an "unplugged" life instead of drawing upon all the free "spiritual electricity" God offers you through His Spirit?

Why? Perhaps it's simply because commitment to Christ requires that we get off our blessed assurance and *do* something—

And quitting is so easy.

An Unstoppable Young Man

Throughout history, there have been many examples of people who refused to quit, who remained committed to a cause—even though their cause was far less meaningful and consequential than the cause of Christ. We can learn a great deal from these people who have set inspiring examples of perseverance and endurance. One such example was a young man from the Midwest named Walter.

In May 1922, at the age of twenty, Walter started his own motion picture company in Kansas City, Missouri. Though he had no money, he raised capital by getting several local investors to purchase $15,000 worth of stock. He hired ten employees and began turning out advertising films that played in the local theaters. Soon, he landed a contract to produce cartoons that were distributed across the country.

Unfortunately, Walter was not much of a businessman.

After all, at age twenty, he had a great deal of youthful exuberance but absolutely no experience running a business.

By the end of 1922, with his company approaching bankruptcy, Walter began cutting salaries and laying off employees. He gave up his own apartment and lived out of a suitcase in his office. Once a week, for a dime, he took a bath at the railroad station. With these cost-cutting measures, he was able to keep his filmmaking business afloat through mid-1923, but when the landlord of his office building evicted him and he had no other place to set up shop, Walter knew it was over.

In July 1923, Walter filed for bankruptcy. Just twenty-one years old, he had already experienced a devastating, humiliating business failure. That same month, he sold his movie camera for $40 and used the money to buy a train ticket to California. He boarded the train carrying a cardboard suitcase and a can of film, all he had left after the bankruptcy proceedings.

Arriving in Hollywood, he tried to get a job as a movie director, applying at every studio in town. No one would hire him. The only film-related job he was able to find was as a movie extra in a Western. The day Walter arrived on the set, the scheduled film shoot was canceled due to rain. "That was the end of my career as an actor," Walter later recalled.

He rented a room at his uncle's house for $5 a week and started drawing animated cartoons. After he sold his first animated cartoon to a New York distributor, Walter borrowed $500 from his uncle and $200 from his brother and started a new studio in Los Angeles. He hired a new staff and turned out films that mixed cartoons with live actors. Later, he came up with the idea for a new cartoon character, Oswald the Lucky Rabbit, which debuted in 1927.

The Oswald cartoons became popular—so popular, in fact, that Walter's distributor went behind his back, hired away Walter's staff of artists, and used a deceptive clause in the contract to steal the Oswald character away from him. For the second time in just four years, Walter was left with nothing and was forced to start over from scratch.

During a train ride from New York to Los Angeles, Walter came up with an idea for a new cartoon character, inspired by a mouse that had lived in a hole in the wall of his Kansas City studio. Back in the days when Walter was living out of a suitcase in that studio, he had fed and befriended that mouse, naming it Mortimer. So, naturally, he decided that his new cartoon character would be called Mortimer Mouse.

Walter's wife, Lillian, convinced him to change Mortimer's name to Mickey—and the rest is history. Or, I should say, *Disney* history. Because Walter, of course, was Walt Disney, and his little cartoon studio grew to become a global media empire.[3]

But it never would have happened if a young man named Walter had been stopped by bankruptcy or by being cheated out of his creation. The Disney empire exists today because a determined young man in his twenties refused to quit.

Now, this was a man who would not give up—over a *cartoon character*! He persevered in his convictions about a series of ink drawings on celluloid! If this man could be so intensely committed to a character in a drawing, shouldn't we be at least as committed to the eternal destiny of human souls? Shouldn't we be at least as committed to leading people out of darkness and sin into the light of eternal life?

What can we learn from Walt Disney that we can apply to our lives? We can learn to see obstacles not as a dead end, but merely as a detour. We can learn to see opposition not as an undertaker, but as a teacher. We can learn to see resistance as a motivation for persistence.

And we can learn that if we refuse to quit, there is no limit to what God can accomplish through our lives.

The Church Is Not Your Mission Field

Take another look at the opening words of Joshua 18: "The whole assembly of the Israelites gathered at Shiloh and set up the Tent of Meeting there." The Tent of Meeting was Israel's house of worship. Joshua knew that worship was essential to the life of the nation of Israel. He understood that a worship experience is needed to uplift, challenge, and motivate God's people. So, when Joshua brought the people of Israel together at Shiloh to claim their inheritance, he began by calling them to worship.

Embedded in these opening lines of Joshua 18 is a principle that I believe is very important for our lives today. The principle is this: God's ultimate goal for our lives as Christians is not to get us to go to church but to move us out into the world. Now, don't misunderstand me: He *does* want us to attend church. He wants us to spend regular time in worshiping Him, and in fellowship with His people.

The problem for many Christians is that their Christian experience begins and ends in church! They seem to think that their mission as Christians is to occupy a certain pew in a certain building every Sunday morning. My friend, the church is not your mission field. Your mission field starts the moment you walk out the door of your church and onto the street. Your mission field is the neighborhood where you live, the office or factory where you work, or the campus where you go to school.

What, then, is worship for? Worship should inspire and empower you as you humbly bow your heart before your awesome Lord. Worship should challenge, encourage, and motivate you as you hear the preaching of His Word. Worship should both convict you and revitalize your heart as you sing hymns of praise to your God. Worship should connect your heart to the heart of God through prayer. Worship should instruct and equip you as you study God's Word with other believers.

So then, worship should inspire, empower, challenge, encourage, motivate, convict, revitalize, connect, instruct, and equip you to go out into your mission field and claim your inheritance from the Lord. What is that inheritance? Your inheritance is your God-given "territory"—that is, your opportunities for witnessing and reaching others for Christ. Your inheritance is all of the people God has placed in your path— your neighbors, your coworkers, your fellow students, your professors and coaches. The people you meet each day are your inheritance. All who need to know that Jesus forgives the repentant sinner, that Jesus restores the brokenhearted, that Jesus redeems the least and the last and the lost—these are your inheritance.

Jesus is knocking at the doors of their hearts. And when they open that door a crack to see who is there, Jesus speaks to them through you and me as we share His message of good news.

Make Your Social Life Count

Look again at the meeting where Joshua gathers the people in Shiloh to worship the Lord. He did exactly what Christian ministers need to do in their churches. He called the people together and he said to them, "Don't let your inheritance go unclaimed! Don't let God's power and blessing in your life go to waste! Don't let the busyness of this world keep you from your mission field! Don't let the worries and weariness of this world keep you from living as a true apostle for your Lord, wherever you work, live, or play! Don't quit! Keep on keeping on with God!"

We all have social lives, leisure lives, times of kicking back and relaxing with friends. Exercise time at the gym. Chats over the back fence. Shopping with friends at the mall. Dinner out, followed by a movie or a concert. We each have a social life. But as Christians, our social lives should not be without purpose. We should care enough about the people we spend time with to talk to them about what's true and what's real.

And what's true and real is Jesus the Lord.

So enjoy your social life. Enjoy your leisure time. But don't forget to make those times count for God.

Nature Abhors a Vacuum

Again, listen to the exasperation and intensity in Joshua's voice as he pleads with the people, "How long will you wait before you begin to take possession of the land that the LORD, the God of your fathers, has given you?" (Josh. 18:3).

In other words, he is telling the people, "Every day you delay in taking possession of the land is a day lost in accomplishing God's plan for the nation of Israel. Every hour that you delay brings us one hour closer to calamity if the enemy returns and becomes reentrenched in the land. Everything we have accomplished by God's power could be lost if you do not claim your inheritance."

There is a scientific dictum, first expressed by Aristotle in 350 BC, that states, "Nature abhors a vacuum." In other words, a completely empty space is unnatural because nature will try to fill that space if it can. For example, if you create a vacuum inside a bottle, nature will try to fill the bottle with air if it can. You can maintain a vacuum in the bottle as long as it is perfectly sealed. The moment the bottle is punctured, even if the puncture is as small as a pinhole, air molecules will rush into the bottle. The vacuum will be replaced by air within seconds.

The same is true in the spiritual realm. Spiritual nature abhors a vacuum. Jesus expressed this principle when He said:

> When an evil spirit comes out of a man, it goes through arid places seeking rest and does not find it. Then it says, "I will return to the house I left." When it arrives, it finds the house unoccupied, swept clean and put in order. Then it goes and takes with it seven other spirits more wicked than itself, and they go in and live there. And the final condition of that man is worse than the first. That is how it will be with this wicked generation.
>
> (Matt. 12:43–45)

In more than three decades of ministry, I have seen this spiritual principle at work in a variety of ways. Jesus is telling us that when a person comes to Christ, there is a moment when all of the old evil is cast out of that person's heart. That is the crucial moment when a person must fill his or her life with the Holy Spirit. That is the crucial moment when that person must claim his or her inheritance in Christ. The life of that person must be filled with God, with worship, with

Christian fellowship, with Bible study, with witnessing and sharing Christ with others. If that person allows a spiritual vacuum to exist in his or her life—*look out!*

Yes, at the moment of conversion, the evil spirit has been cast out—but that evil spirit hasn't gone far. It is watching. It sees that this person has never claimed the promises of God, has never claimed the empowerment of the Holy Spirit, has never claimed the inner filling of the Spirit, has never claimed his or her inheritance in Christ.

And if that evil spirit sees a vacuum in that person's life, it will return. It will reinfest that life. And Jesus said that the evil spirit will not come back alone. It will bring seven more spirits, and that person's spiritual state will be worse than ever before.

I have seen people cry tears of regret because they failed to fill the spiritual vacuum in their lives. They made a commitment to Christ at one point in their lives, but they never claimed their inheritance in Christ. As a result of that vacuum, their lives became filled with sin, addiction, broken relationships, bitterness, resentment, sorrow, regret, and shame. That is what happens if you claim to come to Christ but never claim your inheritance in Christ. That is what happens if you neglect to claim the Lord's power over sin and temptation in your life.

If you leave a spiritual vacuum in your life, it's just a matter of time before your life is reoccupied with the same old sins and habits that plagued you before your conversion. If you do not repent and fill that vacuum with the Lord's Spirit, then it's just a matter of time before your heart becomes so hardened that nothing will soften it or penetrate it. It's just a matter of time before powerful evil forces once again occupy your life and fill you with resentment toward God and resistance to anyone who speaks His truth.

I have seen this principle at work in the lives of people I have known. It is heartbreaking to behold. And that is why I say to you, making the same appeal that Joshua made to his people, "Don't let one more day go by without claiming your rightful place as the Lord's ambassador, your rightful authority in Christ, your rightful victory through Christ, and your rightful inheritance with Christ."

Persistence Pays Off

Every schoolchild knows that Christopher Columbus (1451–1506) was the explorer who discovered America on behalf of Spain while searching for a western route to Asia. But few people realize all the difficulties Columbus had to overcome in order to realize his dream.

He first presented his plans to King John II of Portugal in 1485, but the king considered his ideas to be foolish and unrealistic. So Columbus offered his plans to Italy and England, to no avail.

Next, Columbus presented his plans to King Ferdinand and Queen Isabella, monarchs of Spain. They were baffled by the maps and sketches presented by this crazy dreamer who claimed that it was possible to go east by sailing west. So they referred Columbus's ideas to a committee.

The committee members did what committee members always do: They studied the proposal to death! They spent five years examining the proposal. Throughout those five years, Columbus continued to inquire and plead and coax, trying to get the committee to render a positive verdict. Finally, the committee returned with a consensus: "The idea is impractical."

Accepting the committee's advice, Ferdinand and Isabella rejected the venture. However, they decided to pay Columbus an annual stipend of about $1,000 a year—just to keep him from taking his ideas to another country. This small gesture gave Columbus hope, and he continued to urge Ferdinand and Isabella to reconsider. But the king and queen were occupied with the war against the Moors in southern Spain, so they continued to put Columbus off.

In early 1492, Columbus heard that the Moors had surrendered at Granada. So he sent messages to the king and queen of Spain, begging them to hear him once more. They agreed to receive him at their castle in Córdoba. This time, Isabella and Ferdinand could not agree about whether or not to support Columbus. Isabella, on the advice of her personal priest-confessor, at first refused Columbus's plea, and Columbus actually left the castle thinking he had failed for the final time. But Ferdinand intervened and convinced Isabella to provide the funding he sought.

Finally, Columbus left the court of Ferdinand and Isabella with the promise of three ships, and the money, supplies, and crewmen to carry out his expedition. Persistence had finally paid off.[4]

The history of the world might have turned out differently if Columbus had not been a man of perseverance. He achieved his dream and discovered a new world because he refused to quit. The lesson of his life is clear: When you encounter resistance, try persistence. Never give up.

What if God gave up on you? What if God gave up on me? You and I are believers today because God persisted and pursued us for years before we gave our lives to Him. He did not give up on us. And we must not quit on Him. He has given us a wonderful inheritance, and now it is up to us to move in and occupy it.

Remember the words of Joshua: "How long will you wait before you begin to take possession of the land that the LORD, the God of your fathers, has given you?" (Josh. 18:3).

How long until you claim the precious inheritance that the Lord has given you, my friend? How long?

11

You Want Me to Be a Runner to the City of Refuge?

Joshua 20

$\mathbf{A}$s a boy, I got into my share of mischief. My father was (to put it mildly) long on justice and short on mercy. On those few occasions when I received mercy for my transgressions, it was always at the insistence of my mother. So when I knew that I was about to land in trouble, my first, last, and only instinct was to run from my father—as far as I could and as fast as I could.

I'm not saying my father was abusive or unfair. I must admit that, on those occasions when he disciplined me, I richly deserved my punishment. Unfortunately, as painful as the punishment was, the lesson never seemed to stick with me. The temptation I faced always proved stronger than my fear of my father's wrath. So I incurred his wrath with alarming regularity!

During those years, I had a friend who sometimes got into mischief with me. And there was something about my young friend that continually baffled me. When he got in trouble, he didn't run *away* from his father as I did. Instead, he ran *to* his father! That made no sense to me. It seemed like a totally deranged thing to do! His inexplicable response to his father troubled me for a long time.

Only when I committed my life to Christ did I finally understand the difference between his relationship with his father and my relationship with mine. When I became a Christian, I began to develop an intimate relationship with my heavenly Father. I discovered what it means to have a merciful Father. And that's when I understood that my friend's relationship with his father was actually a picture of what our relationship with our heavenly Father is supposed to be.

Human Fathers and the Heavenly Father

I've been in the ministry for well over thirty years, and I've had the opportunity to talk to countless people through the years. During that time, I've observed that there are two types of people: First, there are those who are like I was when I was a boy. When they fall into sin and disobedience, they run *away* from their heavenly Father. Second, there are those who are like my boyhood friend. As soon as they feel the conviction of sin in their consciences, they run *to* their heavenly Father.

What makes the difference between these two kinds of people? The answer is simple—it all depends on one's view of the heavenly Father.

If you view Him as a vindictive, arbitrary, angry God who is just waiting to let you have it for all your sins, then you will run away from Him. You won't go to Him for forgiveness, because you don't expect Him to forgive you. You expect Him to punish you.

But if you see your heavenly Father as the God of mercy and grace, slow to anger and full of compassion—then of course you will run into His arms for forgiveness.

Here's the problem. Many people unconsciously equate their relationship with their heavenly Father with their relationship with their earthly fathers. Those of us who have had harsh and stern earthly fathers often assume that our heavenly Father is the same way. What a tragic mistake!

Whether your earthly father was gentle or harsh, merciful or stern, don't confuse him with your Father in heaven. There is only one way you can truly know your heavenly Father as He truly is, and that is through His Word. There is only one human manifestation of God the Father, and that is His Son, the Lord Jesus Christ. We see this principle clearly in a scene from John's Gospel.

In that scene, Jesus tells His disciples, "I am the way and the truth and the life. No one comes to the Father except through me" (John 14:6).

Hearing these words, one of the disciples, Philip, says, "Lord, show us the Father and that will be enough for us" (14:8).

And Jesus replies, "Don't you know me, Philip, even after I have been among you such a long time? Anyone who has seen me has seen the Father" (14:9).

If we want to know what God the Father is truly like, all we have to do is look at Jesus, who came to earth as fully God and fully Man—the personification of grace and truth. Through Him, we know that our heavenly Father loves us and cares for us more than any earthly father could. As the nineteenth-century abolitionist minister Henry Ward Beecher remarked, "There is no creature so poor or so low, that he may not look up with childlike confidence to the Creator of the universe and exclaim, 'You are my Father!'"

Now, as we come to Joshua chapter 20, we catch a glimpse of the truly glorious character of our Father in heaven.

Cities of Refuge

Throughout the book of Joshua, we have seen how God relates to His children—in this case, the children of Israel. We have seen God provide for His children in many amazing ways. He has supernaturally led them across the river of impossibility. He has supernaturally demolished the fortified walls of Jericho. He has shown them that they need to remove sin from their midst. In the face of overwhelming odds, He has given them victory after victory over their enemies.

Finally, He has divided the land of promise among the people, and He has gently and mercifully rebuked them when they delayed in claiming their inheritance. Now, in Joshua 20, Israel's merciful heavenly Father instructs the people in how to exercise justice and compassion. He does this by directing the Israelites to designate six cities of refuge.

The cities of refuge were not a new idea that the Lord introduced to the Israelites after they settled in the promised land. God had told people of His plan for cities of refuge even while Israel was still wandering in the wilderness. The first mention is in Exodus, where God says that if a man commits unintentional manslaughter, "he is to flee to a place I will designate" (Exod. 21:13).

The reference to cities of refuge is more detailed and explicit in the book of Numbers:

Six of the towns you give the Levites will be cities of refuge, to which a person who has killed someone may flee. . . . They will be places of refuge from the avenger, so that a person accused of murder may not die before he stands trial before the assembly. These six towns you give will be your cities of refuge. Give three on this side of the Jordan and three in Canaan as cities of refuge. These six towns will be a place of refuge for Israelites, aliens and any other people living among them, so that anyone who has killed another accidentally can flee there.

(35:6, 12-15)

Another detailed description of the cities of refuge and their function in Israelite society is found in Deuteronomy 19:1-13. And finally, here in Joshua 20, the command to designate cities of refuge is repeated a fourth time:

The LORD said to Joshua: "Tell the Israelites to designate the cities of refuge, as I instructed you through Moses, so that anyone who kills a person accidentally and unintentionally may flee there and find protection from the avenger of blood.

"When he flees to one of these cities, he is to stand in the entrance of the city gate and state his case before the elders of that city. Then they are to admit him into their city and give him a place to live with them. If the avenger of blood pursues him, they must not surrender the one accused, because he killed his neighbor unintentionally and without malice aforethought. He is to stay in that city until he has stood trial before the assembly and until the death of the high priest who is serving at that time. Then he may go back to his own home in the town from which he fled."

So they set apart Kedesh in Galilee in the hill country of Naphtali, Shechem in the hill country of Ephraim, and Kiriath Arba (that is, Hebron) in the hill country of Judah. On the east side of the Jordan of Jericho they designated Bezer in the desert on the plateau in the tribe of Reuben, Ramoth in Gilead in the tribe of Gad, and Golan in Bashan in the tribe of Manasseh. Any of the Israelites or any alien living among them who killed someone accidentally could flee to these designated cities and not be killed by the avenger of blood prior to standing trial before the assembly.

(20:1-9)

The command to designate cities of refuge is repeated four times in four different books of the Old Testament. Why does God place so much stress on these cities of refuge? It's because God wants the people of Israel to know that human life is sacred and He desires that His people show mercy to one another. He wants to impress upon His people the value that He places on every human life.

It's a serious thing to take another human life, and murder shall not be tolerated among God's people. But sometimes, accidents take place and people are killed unintentionally. God wants His people to understand that there is a difference between intentional murder and unintentional manslaughter. The murderer and the unintentional manslayer should not be treated the same way.

Hope for the Manslayer

Let's look at the background of God's command regarding cities of refuge. First, we must understand that the Law of Moses requires an eye for an eye, a life for a life. Capital punishment was instituted under the Law of Moses. Why? To underscore the value of human life.

Some would see this as contradictory. How can you teach the value of life by killing someone? But looked at another way, the point becomes clear: The Law was telling the people of Israel, in effect, "The life of your neighbor is so sacred that if you take your neighbor's life away from him by an act of murder, you must pay the ultimate penalty—the forfeiture of your own life."

The problem was that human emotion could sometimes negate God's law. For example, two men might be in the forest cutting wood. One man swings his ax, and the ax-head flies off, striking and killing the other man. Clearly, there was no murderous intent. This was an accident, and the man who committed unintentional manslaughter should not be put to death for an accident. But the dead man's brother might, in a fit of irrational anger, say, "I don't care if it was an accident or not! This man killed my brother, and I want my revenge!"

So God, who is both the God of justice and the God of mercy, said in effect, "Build six cities throughout Israel—three cities on the east side of the river Jordan and three cities on the west. They shall be cities of refuge, and when a man commits unintentional manslaughter, he can go to one of those cities and find sanctuary and protection from any avenger."

But that's not all God commanded. He also said that the roads to the cities of refuge must be kept in good condition. The crossroads had to be well marked. And God commanded that signposts be placed, boldly marked "REFUGE!"

And even that is not all God commanded. He also said that runners were to be stationed along the pathway to guide the fugitive to the city of refuge. The runners would lead the fugitive to the gates of the city of refuge, and they would support him until he reached the city of refuge. And when the fugitive entered the city, he would be taken—probably drenched in sweat and out of breath—to the city elders, who were the legal authority, the court of law, for the city. There the fugitive would present his case to the elders. The elders would make a provisional decision to grant asylum to the accused man until a proper trial could be held.

If the manslayer was acquitted of premeditated murder, he was to live in the city of refuge until the death of the high priest. After the death of the high priest, the manslayer would be free to go home to his community and his family, and he could live there in freedom.

The Great High Priest

At this point, you may say, "I followed God's logic about the cities of refuge until we got to the part about the death of the high priest. Why is the manslayer freed only after the death of the high priest?"

This aspect of God's command about the cities of refuge probably baffled the Old Testament Israelites as well. They must have wondered, *What does the death of the high priest have to do with the freedom of the fugitive?*

But with the benefit of New Testament hindsight, this all makes sense. The death of the high priest is the only ransom that can be paid for the act of manslaughter. The death of the high priest was the only redemption for the guilt of accidentally taking a human life. The death of the high priest was the only atonement for the sin of the fugitive, and the only satisfaction for the demands of justice.

Even though the manslayer was not guilty of murder, he

was guilty of sin. He had taken an innocent life. Someone was dead because of his unintentional actions.

Where there is sin, there is guilt. In order for the fugitive to be free, there must be an atonement. At this point, you may already be sensing where God's logic is leading—and if you haven't already begun to shout for joy, you soon will! God's command about the cities of refuge is profoundly meaningful for your life and mine.

You and I are guilty people. We were born guilty because we have inherited the sin of Adam. We are guilty because we have broken the law of God. We are guilty by living only for ourselves, while ignoring our righteous and holy God. We are guilty of disobedience and insubordination to our Creator.

Whether we have sinned against God out of ignorance or out of deliberate rebellion makes no difference. The courts of heaven have convened and have pronounced us all guilty as charged.

But a runner along the way has told us where we can find refuge, relief from guilt and judgment, and escape from our adversary and accuser. The runner has not only told us where the city of refuge can be found, but who the city of refuge is.

So we come to the city of refuge, and there we are set free, not only from sin but from the wages of sin, which is death. And we receive atonement and redemption and complete liberation. Why? Because our great High Priest has died for us. He has been nailed to a cross on a hill called Calvary.

And now that we have been redeemed, we have become the runners ourselves. We are the ones who point the way to the city of refuge. We are the ones who tell others how to find escape from sin and judgment and everlasting death. We were once refugees. Now God calls us to be runners, pointing guilty fugitives to the city of refuge and to the great High Priest who can set them free.

The death of the great High Priest has set us free from the curse of sin. There is now no condemnation for us. We have been given a new life, eternal life, and God calls us to share this good news with everyone we meet along the way.

In Psalm 46:1, the psalmist looked forward to the place of refuge that God would provide through the death of the Great High Priest: "God is our refuge and strength, an ever-present help in trouble." And while the psalmist looked forward to the death of the great High Priest, the apostle Paul was able to look back to that same event and say, "Therefore, there is now no condemnation for those who are in Christ Jesus" (Rom. 8:1). And the writer to the Hebrews was able to write that we "have fled for refuge to lay hold upon the hope set before us" (Heb. 6:18 KJV).

No one who is in Christ Jesus, who has fled to Him for refuge, has anything to fear from the judgment to come. Notice, I did not say that you have nothing to fear if you attend church, or if you belong to a certain denomination, or if you observe certain religious rites and rituals. The only city of refuge we have is the Lord Jesus Himself. If you are in Christ Jesus, you have refuge and asylum; but as long as you remain outside of Him, you are under judgment. The good news is that you can go to Him for refuge today, at this very moment.

My friend, if you are in the church but have never entered the city of refuge, please listen carefully to what I'm about to tell you: If you have heard the gospel again and again, but you have never responded and have never gone in repentance to Jesus Christ for mercy, forgiveness, and refuge, then you have the most to fear from God's judgment. Why? Because you are responsible for the truth that you have heard. Those who have heard the truth, but have refused to act upon it, will be judged more severely than those who have never heard. To whom much has been given, much shall be required.

The Poison of Sin

Please understand this: The church is not the city of refuge. The church is merely the signpost that points the way to refuge. The church calls out to fugitives, "Flee to Christ! Take refuge in Him!" Only when you flee to Jesus, the Great High Priest who died for you, will you find freedom from guilt, power over sin, and peace in the midst of trouble.

So I ask you: When you feel convicted of sin, when you know that you are in trouble with your heavenly Father, which way do you run? Do you run *away* from your heavenly Father, as I ran away from my earthly father when I was a boy? Or do you run *to* Him, seeking refuge and forgiveness and healing? Do you fear His wrath—or do you long for His mercy?

When you have sinned, do you avoid the church and the fellowship of other Christians? Do you fear that the sermon and the hymns in the worship service will make you feel guilty and fearful of God's judgment?

Or do you eagerly go to church to receive a cleansing message of the mercy and grace of God? Do you long to be in the fellowship of other people who have found refuge in Jesus, the great High Priest?

Do you run to your city of refuge—or are you running away?

In his book *A Daily Passage Through Mark*, author and pastor John R. Wayland tells the story of the 1981 theft of a Volkswagen Beetle somewhere in California—a story that was reported on the national news media. Of course, hundreds of cars are stolen every day in California. Why would the theft of one particular VW Bug become a national news story?

Answer: a box of crackers.

You see, the owner of the car had laced the crackers with rat poison and planned to set the crackers out as bait to kill rodents. After the car was stolen, the owner and the police wanted to apprehend the thief—not merely to recover the car, but to save the thief from being poisoned![1]

I don't know if the thief was ever apprehended—Pastor Wayland doesn't tell us in his book. But I do know that many people are like that car thief. They are on the run from God. They fear His punishment. They are doing everything possible to avoid Him and elude Him—yet all God wants to do is rescue them from the deadly poison of sin! Instead of running from God, we need to run to Him for refuge.

What Kind of Friend . . . ?

And what if God is already your refuge? In that case, I have a question for you: Are you a runner for God? Are you pointing the way to other fugitives so that they can find their city of refuge?

Every day, you encounter people who are fugitives from judgment, their backs breaking under a load of sin. They are desperate to find a place of refuge. They are desperate for mercy, healing, and forgiveness. You know the way to the city of refuge. Have you told anyone else? Or have you kept the good news all to yourself?

You have friends. You share meals with them. You go to movies and concerts with them. Have you ever told them about the city of refuge? Have you ever shared with them the good news of Jesus Christ? If you have been silent, if you've told no one, if you've never pointed the way to refuge and healing, then you have to ask yourself: *What kind of friend am I?*

So which shall it be? Will you accept God's call to be a runner along the way—or will you abandon your post? Are you pointing the way to the city of refuge—or have you lost your way?

Don't let another moment pass without settling that question between you and God.

12

You Want Me to Tell the Story?

Joshua 21–24

Imagine with me a frightening scenario.

You wake up one morning and there is no dawn. By 9:00 a.m., you look out your window and there is not a ray of sunshine. By noon, you step outside and you see that the world is still as black as midnight.

The hours crawl by. Your neighbors huddle in the streets with candles and flashlights. "What's happening?" they ask. "Where is the sun?" Like the wind that rattles the shivering trees, you feel a cold chill of dread running through you. You wonder, *Will the sun ever return?*

By evening, the churches are thronged with worried, frightened people. Some who were thoughtlessly blaspheming God's name just yesterday now cry out to Him, pleading with Him to return the sun to the sky. And you are there with the rest of them, praying to God and wondering if this is some final judgment He has inflicted on the world.

After an all-night prayer meeting, you walk out into the street and you check your watch. It's 5:30 a.m. You think, *On a normal day, the sun would be coming up soon.* And you look to the east—

And you think you see a faint smudge of light peeking up over the horizon. You're not sure if you dare believe what you see. You stare toward the eastern sky for a few minutes longer until you are sure. Yes, you definitely see a few rays of sunlight over the horizon. You're sure now. A new day is dawning.

You turn to the other people who have emerged from the church and you shout, "The sun is rising! The sun is rising!"

And in moments, shouts of joy and excitement fill the air. People come out of their homes and fill the streets as the sky slowly turns from black to indigo to blue. Your neighbors turn their faces to the warmth of the rising sun.

After twenty-four hours of darkness and dread, you and everyone around you join in praise to God. Why? Because it's morning and the sun has risen.

Now let me ask you a question. The sun rises every morning—why don't we praise God every single day for the sun? Why don't we all feel excited and elated just to awaken each morning to a new day? Why don't we have an attitude of grateful praise every day for the creation all around us and for the blessings God has given us? Why would we praise God only after going through a frightful experience?

The answer is obvious. We take God and all of His gifts for granted. It seems that we don't truly appreciate what we have until we lose it.

We are a forgetful people.

Spiritual Amnesia

God understands that we are forgetful by nature. And that is why, in His Word, God tells us repeatedly, from Genesis to Revelation, "Remember!"

"*Remember* that you were slaves in Egypt and that the LORD your God brought you out of there with a mighty hand and an outstretched arm" (Deut. 5:15, emphasis added). "*Remember* the LORD your God, for it is he who gives you the ability to produce wealth" (Deut. 8:18, emphasis added). "*Remember* the former things, those of long ago; I am God, and there is no other; I am God, and there is none like me" (Isa. 46:9, emphasis added). "*Remember* the law of my servant Moses, the decrees and laws I gave him at Horeb for all Israel" (Mal. 4:4, emphasis added).

"*Remember* the words I spoke to you: 'No servant is greater than his master'" (John 15:20, emphasis added). "*Remember* that at that time you were separate from Christ, excluded from citizenship in Israel and foreigners to the covenants of the promise, without hope and without God in the world" (Eph. 2:12, emphasis added). "*Remember* the height from which you have fallen! Repent and do the things you did at first" (Rev. 2:5, emphasis added).

Remember! Remember! Remember! God knows that we are a forgetful people, and so He calls us, again and again, to *remember.* It's as if the entire human race is afflicted with amnesia.

I'm sure you know that amnesia is a medical condition involving a loss of memory. Hollywood has trivialized amnesia in many TV shows and motion pictures. A character in the show gets conked on the head and instantly forgets who he is, where he lives, and what his own name is—and then that situation is exploited for laughs.

But in real life, amnesia is a serious medical condition. A person with amnesia may have brain damage due to disease, trauma, or drugs. The amnesia victim may forget many significant details about his life, including his identity, for a period of hours or years, or even for life. An amnesia victim is often unable to remember even the most significant milestones in her life, such as the birth of a child or a wedding day. These important memories have simply been blotted out of the mind by the medical condition called "amnesia."

There is a spiritual equivalent of amnesia. The spiritual form is far more common than physical amnesia. Spiritual amnesia occurs when we forget the Lord's past blessings and mercies as if we had never received them. It happens when we allow our present troubles and afflictions to blot out our memory of all the times we have experienced God's goodness, His faithfulness, His provision, and His unmerited favor and grace.

We are like the man who went to his doctor and said, "Doc, can you help me? I can't remember a thing."

"When did you first become aware of this problem?" the doctor asked.

"What problem?" said the man.

Truth be told, most of us remember what we want to remember. Men in particular are notorious for remembering only what is important to them. They tend to develop temporary amnesia about the things that are important to other people—and especially to their wives. As the saying goes, "It's a 'guy thing.'"

Most men are like the baseball fanatic who had a phenomenal memory for statistics, batting averages, box scores, and player trivia. He could rattle off a staggering volume of baseball knowledge without a moment's hesitation.

A neighbor once said to him, "Your head is crammed so full of baseball information that you've probably forgotten everything else. For example, have you ever forgotten your wedding anniversary?"

"Absolutely not! I couldn't forget my wedding anniversary in a million years! I was married the day Bobby Thompson hit a home run off a pitch by Ralph Branca and won the pennant for the Giants! How could I ever forget my wedding day?"

God knows that we human beings are a race of spiritual amnesiacs. He knows our tendency to forget His goodness and mercy. He knows we are prone to taking His past blessings for granted and presuming on His grace for the future. That's why, in the final chapter of the book of Joshua, He says, in effect, "Don't forget what I've done for you. Don't be ungrateful. Don't take credit for the things I have done for you. Remember Me."

The Significance of Shechem

In the concluding chapters of the book of Joshua, we see that the nation of Israel is at last taking possession of the land and dividing it among the tribes as the Lord commanded. In chapter 20, we saw the designation of cities of refuge.

Then, in Joshua 21, the Israelites set aside towns and pastureland for the priests of the Levite tribe, so that they would have homes and fields for their livestock. The chapter closes with a statement that Israel now enjoys peace and prosperity in fulfillment of the promise that God made to the nation:

So the LORD gave Israel all the land he had sworn to give their forefathers, and they took possession of it and settled there. The LORD gave them rest on every side, just as he had sworn to their forefathers. Not one of their enemies withstood them; the LORD handed all their enemies over to them. Not one of all the LORD's good promises to the house of Israel failed; every one was fulfilled.

(Josh. 21:43–45)

In Joshua 22, Joshua blesses the eastern tribes—the Reubenites, the Gadites, and the tribe of Manasseh—and invites them to settle on the west bank of the Jordan. This chapter also records a misunderstanding over an altar that the eastern tribes built, and how that misunderstanding was resolved and peace was restored.

Then, in Joshua 23, the old warrior Joshua sees that the end of his life is approaching, so he summons the leaders of Israel—the elders, judges, and officials of the tribes—and he reminds them of all that God has done for them:

You yourselves have seen everything the LORD your God has done to all these nations for your sake; it was the LORD your God who fought for you. . . .

Now I am about to go the way of all the earth. You know with all your heart and soul that not one of all the good promises the LORD your God gave you has failed. Every promise has been fulfilled; not one has failed. But just as every good promise of the LORD your God has come true, so the LORD will bring on you all the evil he has threatened, until he has destroyed you from this good land he has given you. If you violate the covenant of the LORD your God, which he commanded you, and go and serve other gods and bow down to them, the LORD's anger will burn against you, and you will quickly perish from the good land he has given you.

(3, 14–16)

So, with the end of his life approaching, Joshua reminds the leaders of the people of the goodness of God and of the fulfillment of all His promises. But Joshua also warns Israel of the consequences if the people ever turn away from God to serve false gods.

And with that, we come to Joshua 24, the last chapter of the book of Joshua. In this concluding chapter, Joshua assembles all the tribes of Israel at a place called Shechem, where the Palestinian village of Nablus stands today. Joshua deliberately chose Shechem as the meeting place because of its profound historical significance to the Israelites. Six centuries earlier, the Lord had appeared to Abraham at Shechem, and there He confirmed His promise to give the land of Canaan to Abraham's descendants.

Six hundred years had passed from the time God made that promise to Abraham until the time it was fulfilled. Six hundred years is a long time to us, but scarcely a tick of the clock to the Creator of the universe. Human beings might forget a promise that was made six centuries earlier, but God never forgets. The promise was confirmed to Abraham at Shechem, and there a grateful Abraham built an altar of worship to the Lord.

It was also at Shechem that Jacob, Abraham's grandson, surrendered and removed the idols so that he could worship the one true God. So Shechem was a place of deep significance—and a place of remembrance.

Now, six hundred years after Abraham, Joshua gathers

Israel at that site to remind the people of the faithfulness of God—the God who never forgets His promises, the God who always keeps His word. And Joshua reminds the people of God's goodness to Israel, year after year, century after century.

Joshua begins by reminding the people that God called Abraham out from among the tribes of idol worshipers beyond the river. God brought Abraham into Canaan and gave him many descendants—Isaac, Jacob, and the children of Jacob who went down into Egypt.

Then Joshua reminds the people how God used Moses and Aaron to deliver the people of Israel out of Egypt; how He vanquished the Egyptians; and how He led the people through the Red Sea and provided for them in the desert. He reminds the people how God gave them the victory over the Canaanites and Amorites and all of their enemies in the land. These victories were won not by the swords and bows of the Israelites, but by the supernatural might of the Lord.

Then Joshua reminds them that God has given them a land on which they have not toiled, cities they have not built, and produce from vineyards and olive groves they did not plant. Everything they have has been given to them by the grace of God. Joshua gives them one reminder after another of God's rich blessing and provision in their lives—and he does so at this historical site called Shechem.

Where Is Your Shechem?

Shechem was Israel's monument of remembrance. We all need a Shechem in our lives. In your life, Shechem may not be a place on the map. Your Shechem may be a place in your mind, a monument in your memory. For each of us, Shechem is that place where God has met us in a special way, and has transformed our lives. It's a place where God has blessed us, provided for us, rescued us, fulfilled His promises to us, answered our prayers, intervened on our behalf, and showed Himself faithful in spite of our unfaithfulness. It's the place where God gave us more grace, even though we deserved condemnation.

We all need a Shechem, a place we can go to remember the goodness, grace, and faithfulness of God.

Remembering—and Responding

God, through Joshua, reminds Israel again and again of how He took them out of the mud pits of their Egyptian slavery, led them through the depths of the Red Sea, supernaturally fed them manna in the wilderness, led them with a pillar of cloud by day and a pillar of fire by night, brought them safely across the river of impossibility, and gave them victory after victory over all of their enemies. Seventeen times in this passage, God reminds the people of what He has done in their lives: "I took . . . I gave . . . I sent . . . I brought . . . I delivered you."

The Lord could well say the same thing to you and me that He said to Israel. He provides us with strength and health. He gives us the ability to earn a living. He gives us our talents and abilities. He provides us with the ability to think, reason, and make decisions. He places us in a land brimming with opportunity. If we suffer injuries or need surgery, He enables our bodies to knit together and heal.

Those children we love and treasure so much are not ours, but His; they are God's gift to us, and we are temporary stewards of that gift. (When they become teenagers, you may question that gift—but enjoy them for now.) Everything we are and everything we have is a gift and a blessing from God.

And that is Joshua's message to the people of Israel. After reminding the Israelites of all the blessings of God, he then reminds them of their responsibility before God. Remembering is not enough. We must also respond to the blessings that God has given us.

What should our response be?

While I was on a book tour in Dallas, a TV interviewer said to me, "You've written a book about an Old Testament character who took a stand for God, and God blessed him and used him in a miraculous way. But that's an old story from the Old Testament. Things like that don't happen anymore, do they?"

For a moment, I wondered how I should answer that question—and then the Lord gave me the words to say. "You have just introduced me," I said, "as someone who is broadcasting the gospel around the world twenty-three hundred times a week. Well, normally I don't like to talk about myself, but I will do so now for the glory of God. I need to tell you something about myself. You are looking at a man who should not be here, except for the grace of God. Before I was born, my mother had serious health problems, and the doctor had decided that I should be aborted. It was only a miracle of God that enabled me to live.

"I grew up in the Middle East, as a Christian in a Christian home surrounded by a Muslim culture. Even though I didn't always behave like a Christian, my first name, Michael, marked me as coming from a Christian family. So, during the first nineteen years of my life, I grew up knowing what it feels like to be persecuted for Christ.

"I had very low self-esteem as a young man. I didn't feel

that I had any talents or abilities. I certainly had no writing or speaking ability. At the age of twenty, I could not even put two sentences together. When I was twenty-two, I took pen and paper and made a list of my assets and liabilities. I could easily think of all my flaws and defects. My list of liabilities was so long that I couldn't fit them all on one page—I had to continue the list on another page.

"And my list of assets? The sheet was blank. I couldn't think of one. I didn't think that God had given me a single gift that I could use for Him. I was painfully shy. I saw myself as a nothing, a nobody. I had nothing to offer God but my useless self.

"But I said to Jesus, 'Lord, I know You died on the cross for me. I know You saved me from the wages of sin. You gave me Your all, and I have nothing to give to You. All I have to give to You is my all, which is next to nothing. Use me in whatever way You want.'

"And today, twenty-three hundred times a week, the gospel of Jesus Christ is being broadcast to millions of people in more than 190 countries. God took all that I am, which is next to nothing, and He has done something extraordinary. You said you don't think that God still blesses people and uses people the way He did in the Old Testament. I stand here today, living proof that He still does."

A long time ago, I made an amazing discovery: God is not looking for *abilities*. He's looking for *availability*. God wants to know how you and I will respond to His grace and blessings.

It's important for us to remember what God has done for us in the past. It's important for us to review our blessings and to say, "Thank You, God, for all of Your blessings." But we mustn't stop there. God wants to know how we are going to *respond* to His blessings. He wants us to offer Him our all—even if our all is nearly a zero.

We need to continually remind ourselves of our responsibility to God for all the good things He has given us. It's important to be grateful, but saying, "Thank You, God," is meaningless if we are not willing to demonstrate our gratitude by the way we live our lives.

God has blessed us richly so that we may become witnesses and ambassadors for Him. He has blessed us so that He can send us out into the world to share the good news of Jesus Christ with everyone we meet.

When Jesus responded in obedience to the call of the Father, He did something costly. He paid a great price. It was a price He did not have to pay, but one He freely chose to pay. Being fully God, Jesus could have shouted down from heaven, "Believe!" He could have appeared in all of His supernatural power and glory to terrify us into worshiping, accepting, and believing in Him. But that was not His way.

Jesus came down from heaven. He came as a baby. He grew up as one of us, a human being, vulnerable to all the hurts, sorrows, and dangers that afflict us all. He allowed Himself to be nailed to a cross. He allowed His own blood to be spilled. He paid the highest price imaginable to purchase our redemption—a price of suffering and shame, a price of separation from the Father, a price of darkness and death.

And what is our response? Shall we just say, "Thank You," then go on about our lives? Or should our response be costly as well? If we are truly grateful to God for all He has done for us, shouldn't it cost us something to show our gratitude? Shouldn't it cost us all that we have and all that we are?

Joshua's Exasperation

As you read through Joshua 24, you will encounter a section that is surprising, and perhaps a bit troubling. You get the impression that, as Joshua is reminding the people of all that God has done for them, their response is tepid and lacking in enthusiasm. If you have ever spoken in public, then you know how easy it is to read the emotions of an audience. You can tell whether they are responding eagerly to your words—or whether they are not taking your message seriously.

And it seems to me that, as Joshua spoke to the people of Israel, he saw their responses on their faces and in their body language. He saw that some of them were yawning or scratching their necks. Some were talking among themselves and not paying attention. Some had their arms folded across their chests, as if they were placing a barrier between themselves and Joshua's message.

And Joshua could read these people like a book! He knew what they were thinking. He could see it on their faces—a look that said, "Huh? What's that, Joshua? You want us to do *what*? Oh, yeah, yeah, we heard you. Yeah, okay, we'll serve the Lord. Sure. Whatever you say."

Upon receiving this lukewarm response from the people, Joshua got exasperated and a little hot under the collar. So he ratcheted up his rhetoric. He challenged the people and demanded that they make a decision, right then and there: "Choose for yourselves this day whom you will serve, whether the gods your forefathers served beyond the River, or the gods of the Amorites, in whose land you are living. But as for me and my household, we will serve the LORD" (Josh. 24:15).

Well, now the people began to wake up a bit. They realized

that Joshua meant business, and that he was not happy with their lukewarm response. So they responded, "Far be it from us to forsake the LORD to serve other gods! . . . We too will serve the LORD, because he is our God" (Josh. 24:16, 18).

But Joshua still wasn't satisfied with their response. Perhaps he was still getting a lot of vacant stares from the crowd. Clearly, he felt that the people were not responding out of genuine conviction. They seemed to be saying yes with their mouths but no with their eyes—and their eyes told the truth about their hearts. Joshua would not be satisfied with lip service. He wasn't going to let the people get away with saying, "Yeah, okay, sure, we'll serve Jehovah. We'll go to church when we can. We'll put a few bucks in the offering plate. Sure, Joshua, sure."

So Joshua openly expressed his doubts about the seriousness of their commitment. "You are not able to serve the LORD," Joshua told them. "He is a holy God; he is a jealous God. He will not forgive your rebellion and your sins. If you forsake the LORD and serve foreign gods, he will turn and bring disaster on you and make an end of you, after he has been good to you" (Josh. 24:19–20).

At this point, the people responded even more vehemently: "No! We will serve the LORD" (Josh. 24:21).

Why is Joshua being so hard on the Israelites? They promised to serve the Lord. They promised that they would never serve other gods. Why, then, was Joshua so skeptical toward them? Why did he tell them, "You are not able to serve the LORD"?

I believe that Joshua wanted to impress upon his people the seriousness of this commitment. He was telling them, in effect, "Don't just worship Jehovah halfheartedly. Don't serve

Him out of a sense of obligation. Don't think you can bribe Him to get Him on your good side. Don't just go through the motions of being religious while your heart is set upon the material things in this world."

Joshua knew how fickle and forgetful the human heart can be. He understood that the human race is prone to spiritual amnesia. So he drove the point home as if he were driving a railroad spike with a sledgehammer. He said, in effect, "You people say you're going to serve God. Well, your response right now doesn't exactly inspire my confidence. Maybe you'll keep this covenant—and maybe you won't. Maybe you'll persevere in serving the Lord—or maybe you'll forget your promise and go off after other gods. Well, that's your responsibility. But as far as my family and I are concerned, we will serve the Lord.

"We will serve the Lord regardless of what the opinion polls say. We will serve the Lord regardless of what the culture says. We will serve the Lord regardless of peer pressure. Even if others mock us and ridicule us, we will serve the Lord. In fact, we will serve the Lord even if we are persecuted for our faith. I want nothing to do with halfhearted commitments. My family and I are devoted, body and soul, to serving Jehovah alone. As for me and my house, we will serve the Lord."

The Danger of Idolatry

You may wonder why Joshua places so much emphasis on the question of foreign gods and idols. Why was he so worried that the Israelites would worship idols? After all, the people of Israel had seen many miraculous displays of God's awesome power. They knew that it was Jehovah, the one true God, who had brought them across the river of impossibility, who had collapsed the walls of Jericho, who had delivered all of their enemies into their hands. They had seen miracle after miracle. After everything the Israelites had experienced, did Joshua seriously think that the nation of Israel would turn away from the one true God and begin worshiping idols?

Yes, that's exactly what Joshua thought!

He understood the problem of spiritual amnesia. He knew that the people of Israel had seen the wonders of God before and had still lapsed into idolatry. The Israelite people had been miraculously delivered from bondage in Egypt, had fed on manna in the wilderness, had been led through the desert by a pillar of clouds and a pillar of fire—yet in no time at all, they turned away from God and worshiped a golden calf! So Joshua understood the danger of idolatry.

The sin of idolatry is still a very real danger in our lives today. That probably sounds like a preposterous statement, but it is absolutely true. We Christians have our idols that we worship, and that seduce our hearts away from the one true God. You may not know my idols, and I don't know yours, but we all have them.

Friend in Christ, Joshua is speaking across the centuries to your heart and mine. He is trying to shake us out of our lethargy and our spiritual smugness and our spiritual amnesia. He is shouting to us, "You are not able to serve the Lord! He is a holy God; He is a jealous God! If you forsake Him and allow yourself to be seduced by idols after all the blessings you've received from Him, you will bring disaster upon yourself! Don't worship Jehovah halfheartedly! Don't just go through the motions of being religious while your heart is set upon the material things in this world!"

You must not sit there with this book in your hands, saying, "Yeah, okay, someday I'll follow through on a commitment to serve the Lord. My plate is really full right now, so this is really a bad time for me to fully commit myself to the Lord. But one of these days, when I'm not so busy, I'll definitely make God my top priority."

I can tell you with 100 percent certainty that "one of these days" will never arrive. Whatever you put off until "one of these days," you put off forever. The Scriptures tell us, "[The Lord] says, 'In the time of my favor I heard you, and in the day of salvation I helped you.' I tell you, *now* is the time of God's favor, *now* is the day of salvation" (2 Cor. 6:2, emphasis added).

So make your commitment—*now*. Take a stand—*now*. Demonstrate your allegiance to Christ—*now*. Let your walk match your talk—*now*. Not tomorrow. Not one of these days. Not some time when you're not so busy. *Now.*

You really don't know if you are going to be around tomorrow. You can't even take your next breath, your next heartbeat for granted. You woke up this morning, and God graciously granted you one more day—but there is no guarantee that you will wake up tomorrow.

There is a reason why God has given this day to you—and you had better find out why. Go to Him and ask Him how you can serve Him this day. Ask Him, "Who have You placed in my path today? Who do You want me to talk to today? Who needs to hear what You have done in my life? Who needs to hear the good news of Jesus Christ?"

Ask God these questions, and you will be amazed at the answers He gives you.

A Covenant with God

What is a covenant?

A covenant is a solemn and binding agreement between

two or more persons. Covenants are normally made between two equal parties. For example, in the covenant of marriage, two equal human beings, a man and a woman, make an agreement to live faithfully together as husband and wife.

But in the covenant between God and humanity, the Lord does an amazing and magnificent thing: The perfect, righteous, all-powerful Creator of the universe makes a solemn and binding covenant with the weak, sin-ridden, untrustworthy creatures of His creation. He makes and keeps promises with inferiors.

We serve a covenant-making, covenant-keeping God! The One who long ago said, "Let there be light," now says to the creatures of His creation, "I want to enter into a binding covenant with you."

"We are not worthy," we say.

"Still," God replies, "this is what I desire to do."

Even more important, the covenant God makes with us is not a cold and formal contract, like a business agreement. There are no "wherefores" and "heretofores" or "aforesaids" in God's covenant with us. His covenant is an expression of love from parent to child, as He says through the prophet Isaiah: "Can a mother forget the baby at her breast and have no compassion on the child she has borne? Though she may forget, I will not forget you!" (Isa. 49:15).

What a privilege it is to know that the Creator of the universe seeks fellowship with us, wants to covenant with us, and loves us even more than a mother loves her nursing baby. What a blessing to know that we are the beloved children of our awesome Creator-God!

He has imparted His message to us and has entrusted His

gospel to us. And now He calls us to be a blessing to others, to share His message of love and grace with everyone we meet, so that we might rescue some of those people from sin and death and the oppression of Satan.

Have you entered into a covenant with God? Have you received the salvation that only Jesus Christ can give you? You can enter into this covenant today. Simply go to Him and say with a sincere and trusting heart, "Lord Jesus, come into my life. I've been living apart from You. I've been serving my own interests and living in my own strength. I know that I can't live without You. I acknowledge my sins. Please forgive me and save me from my sins. I thank You for dying on the cross and rising again so that I can live eternally with You."

Pray that prayer. Make that covenant with Him—and He will do it. That is the promise He has made to you, and He will keep it.

A. B. Earle (1812–1895) was an evangelist in nineteenth-century America. Converted to Christ at age sixteen, he became a preacher at eighteen and had a six-decade-long career speaking for the Lord. He held evangelistic meetings in every state of the Union and all across Canada. He also mentored more than four hundred young preachers and wrote numerous Christian books.

Once, while preaching in New London, Connecticut, Earle saw one of the state's most prominent attorneys come in and sit down in an evangelistic service. Though the man had fame, wealth, eloquence, and intelligence, he did not have God in his life. He came to Earle's evangelistic meeting because he knew that he did not have peace with God.

As he spoke, Earle felt God calling him to do something he didn't normally do in an evangelistic service. "Usually," he told the audience, "I invite people to leave their chairs and come forward so I can pray with them to receive Christ. But tonight, I propose that, instead of coming forward, you get out of your chair and kneel down on the floor. Let the act of kneeling before God be the visible symbol of the covenant you now make with Him. Let it be the token of your complete surrender to God—a surrender that you will never revoke, never take back. But kneel only if you intend to make a covenant of total surrender to Him."

As Earle said these words, he saw the prominent attorney shift in his chair as if a great struggle were going on within his soul. The man moved as if to kneel—then he sat back—then moved again toward the floor. And the whole time he was letting himself down to the floor, something seemed to strive within him for control of his body. Something fought him inside and tried to keep his knees from touching the floor. Then—finally—the man was down on his knees! And the struggle ceased.

Earle said the man later told him that "the moment his knee reached the floor, he felt the witness in his heart that he was born again. This action of the will unbolted the door of the heart so that the Spirit entered and imparted life" to the attorney.[1]

How do you experience a saving covenant relationship with the Lord Jesus Christ? By surrendering your will to Him. Unbolt the door of your heart and invite Him in. His Spirit will enter and impart life to you—eternal life through Jesus Christ.

The Greatest Promise of All

The Scriptures tell us that after the people of Israel had confirmed their covenant with the Lord, "Joshua sent the people away, each to his own inheritance. After these things, Joshua son of Nun, the servant of the LORD, died at the age of a hundred and ten. And they buried him in the land of his inheritance, at Timnath Serah in the hill country of Ephraim, north of Mount Gaash" (Josh. 24:28–30).

What a great inheritance Joshua had! And what a legacy he left for you and me. Born a slave in Egypt, he died as an honored and revered leader of a nation. Joshua was a man of optimistic faith who followed his Lord across the river of impossibility into the land of promise. By faith, he saw the walls of Jericho collapse to the ground. By faith, he saw the land of Canaan delivered from idolatry. By faith, he led the people of Israel into a covenant relationship with the Lord their God.

The Lord is a covenant-making, covenant-keeping God. Whether the days are bright and sunny or dark and troubled, He is there. Everything we are and have comes from the Father, and from His Son, Jesus Christ. Our Lord will never forget His promises to us; He fulfills every one. And the greatest promise of all is the promise of the Lord Jesus at the conclusion of Matthew's Gospel:

> All authority in heaven and on earth has been given to me. Therefore go and make disciples of all nations, baptizing them in the name of the Father and of the Son and of the Holy Spirit, and teaching them to obey everything I have commanded you. And surely I am with you always, to the very end of the age.
>
> (Matt. 28:18–20)

Notes

1. You Want Me to Step Up?

1. Clifton Fadiman, "Sir Winston Churchill," *The Little, Brown Book of Anecdotes* (Boston: Little, Brown, 1985), entry 14, 122-23; James Allen Ward: "Recommendation for Honours and Awards," facsimile of original documents supporting recommendation of the Victoria Cross for Sgt. James Allen Ward, National Archives, Great Britain, http://www.nationalarchives.gov.uk/theartofwar/ Popup/AIR_2_5686_WARD.htm and http://www .nationalarchives.gov.uk/theartofwar/Popup/AIR_ 2_5686_2_WARD.htm; author unknown, "The Victoria Cross Awarded to Sergeant James Allen Ward," Victoria Cross Web site, http://www .victoriacross.org.uk/bbwardja.htm; author unknown, "James Allen Ward," VC Recipients, http://www .rafbombercommand.com/people_vcwinners_ citations002.html.
2. H. Richard Niebuhr, *The Kingdom of God in America* (New York: Harper & Brothers, 1937), 193.
3. George G. Hunter III, *The Celtic Way of Evangelism:*

How Christianity Can Reach the West . . . Again (Nashville: Abingdon Press, 2000), 8.

4. Dan Kimball, "I Like Jesus, Not the Church," *Outreach* magazine online, http://outreachmagazine.com/ library/features/MA07ftrILikeJesusNottheChurch .asp.

5. Interview with Art Fowler.

6. Ron Edmonson, "Fellowship, Part 7," Mustard Seed Ministry, http://www.christweb.com/Mustardseed Thoughts/Fellowship,Part7.html.

2. You Want Me to Go into Enemy Territory?

1. Doron Geller, "Eli Cohen," Jewish Virtual Library, http://www.jewishvirtuallibrary.org/jsource/ biography/Eli_Cohen.html; Ella Florsheim and Avi Shilon, "The Handler," *Azure*, Winter 5766 / 2006, no. 23, http://www.azure.org.il/magazine/magazine .asp?id=284; author unknown, "Eli Cohen: Hero of Israel," Save Israel, http://www.saveisrael.com/mar- tyred/elicohen.htm.

2. C. S. Lewis, *Mere Christianity* (New York: Macmil- lan, 1960), 51.

3. Mitsuo Fuchida, "The Enemy Whose Attack Provoked America," http://chi.gospelcom.net/kids/glimpses forkids/gfk029.php.

3. You Want Me to Cross the River of Impossibility?

1. Clifton Fadiman, "Chaim Weizmann," *The Little, Brown Book of Anecdotes* (Boston: Little, Brown, 1985), entry 1, 576; author unknown, "Weizmann, Chaim (1874–1952)," Jewish Agency for Israel, http://

www.jafi.org.il/education/100/people/bios/weiz
.html.

2. George S. Patton, *The Patton Papers,* ed. Martin
Blumenson (Cambridge, MA: Da Capo Press, 1996),
571; Paul W. Powell, *Getting the Lead out of Leadership*, 51, http://www.baylor.edu/truett/pdfs/books/
GettingLeadLeadership.pdf.

3. Kenneth O. Gangel and Max E. Anders, *Holman Old
Testament Commentary: Joshua* (Nashville: Broad-
man, 2002), 53.

4. You Want Me to Yield?

1. Pavel Gireyev, "The Mystery of the Russian Titanic,"
Pravda, December 9, 2003, http://english.pravda
.ru/science/19/94/377/10890_wreckage.html.

2. William Moses Tidwell, *Effective Illustrations*,
"Topic V—Consecration, 030—'Colt and All, Lord'"
http://wesley.nnu.edu/wesleyctr/books/0101-0200/
HDM0165.PDF; author unknown, "Surrender: 'Colt
and All,'" Sermon Illustrations, http://elbourne.org/
sermons/index.mv?illustration+2118.

5. You Want Me to Get with the Program?

1. Bryant Wood and Gary Byer (Associates for Biblical
Research), "Is the Bible Accurate Concerning the
Destruction of the Walls of Jericho?," ChristianAnswers
.net, http://christiananswers.net/q-abr/abr-a011.html.

2. John Noble Wilford, "Believers Score in Battle Over
the Battle of Jericho," *New York Times*, February 22,
1990, http://query.nytimes.com/gst/fullpage.html
?res=9C0CE6D91638F931A15751C0A966958260;

Michael S. Sanders, "Jericho—Part I: Introduction," Mysteries of the Bible, http://www.biblemysteries .com/lectures/jericho.htm.

3. Quoted by David O. Dykes in his sermon "Joshua Didn't Fight the Battle of Jericho," October 11, 1998, Green Acres Baptist Church, Tyler, Texas, http:// www.gabc.org/media/documents/s101198P.pdf.

4. Dr. James D. Price, "Yehoshua, Yeshua or Yeshu: Which Is the Name of Jesus in Hebrew?," http:// www.direct.ca/trinity/yehoshua.html.

5. Posted at http://sermoncrafters.org/ill.cgi?a=b&p= 1&t=B.

6. Porter B. Williamson, *General Patton's Principles for Life and Leadership*, quoted in "Thought for 30 November 2007, General George S. Patton, Jr.," http://budaksenaling.blogspot.com/.

6. You Want Me to Learn from My Mistakes?

1. Stuart A. Herrington, *Traitors Among Us: Inside the Spy Catcher's World* (New York: Harvest, 2000), 388.

2. George Barna, "Americans Donate Billions to Charity, but Giving to Churches Has Declined," Barna Group, April 25, 2005, http://www.barna.org/FlexPage.asp x?Page=BarnaUpdate&BarnaUpdateID=187.

3. Jeremiah Burroughs, "Secret Sins," Great Quotes, http://thequotes.wordpress.com/2007/06/27/secret-sins.

4. Author's paraphrase of public domain text of the *Confessions* of Saint Augustine, Book VIII, from the 1921 Chatto & Windus edition, transl. Edward Bouve-

rie Pusey, http://www.gutenberg.org/dirs/etext02/
tcosa10.txt. Original text reads: "But I wretched,
most wretched, in the very commencement of my
early youth, had begged chastity of Thee, and said,
'Give me chastity and continency, only not yet.' For
I feared lest Thou shouldest hear me soon, and soon
cure me of the disease of concupiscence, which I
wished to have satisfied, rather than extinguished."

7. You Want Me to Learn to Pray for Discernment?

1. Rachel Zoll, "Religion-Related Fraud Getting Worse,"
   Associated Press, August 13, 2006, http://www.reli
   gionnewsblog.com/15614/religion-related-fraud-
   getting-worse.

2. William P. Anderson, "James Bennett Pritchard (4
   October 1909–1 January 1997)," *Proceedings of
   the American Philosophical Society*, vol. 143, no.
   3, September 1999, 474, http://www.aps-pub.com/
   proceedings/1433/Pritchard.pdf.

3. Author unknown, "Genesis 3: Don't Be Deceived!,"
   NETBible: Sermon Illustrations, http://net.bible.org/
   illustration.php?topic=1024.

8. You Want Me to Claim the Total Victory?

1. Bruce Felton, Mark Fowler, *The Best, Worst, and
   Most Unusual* (New York: Galahad, 1994), 406–7;
   Bruce Catton, *Grant Takes Command* (New York:
   Little, Brown & Co., 1968), 320–25; author unknown,
   "Crater," CWSAC Battle Summaries, http://www
   .nps.gov/history/hps/abpp/battles/va070.htm;author
   unknown, "The Battle of the Crater, July 30, 1864,"

NPS Historical Handbook: Petersburg, http://www
.nps.gov/history/history/online_books/hh/13/
hh13f.htm.

2. G. K. Chesterton, *The Everlasting Man* (San Francisco: Ignatius Press, 1993), 145; W. Robertson Smith
and George F. Moore, "Baal," *Encyclopædia Biblica*,
ed. T. K. Cheyne and J. Sutherland Black (London:
Macmillan, 1899), http://www.case.edu/univlib/
preserve/Etana/encyl_biblica_a-d/baal-baca.pdf.

3. Dennis J. De Haan, "Standing Firm," *Our Daily Bread*,
May 3, 1994, http://www.iclnet.org/pub/resources/
text/Our.Daily.Bread/94-2qtr/db940503.TXT.

4. George William Rusden, *History of Australia* (Melbourne: Melville, Mullen & Slade, 1887), 508–10,
http://books.google.com/books?id=QM4ezFbt6BQ
C&pg=PA510&dq=%22Mount+Disappointment%22
+Hume; author unknown, "Mount Disappointment,"
Mount Disappointment, http://www.wandong.org
.au/html/mtdisappointment.html.

9. You Want Me to Trust in the Cosmic Real Estate Developer?

1 Story compiled from the following news reports:
Anderson Cooper 360 Degrees, "Deadly Lessons:
24 Hours in Chicago," aired June 1, 2007, http://tran
scripts.cnn.com/TRANSCRIPTS/0706/01/acd.02
.html; Mai Martinez, Rafael Romo, Dorothy Tucker,
and Dana Kozlov, "Family Mourns Teen Hero Killed
in CTA Bus Shooting," http://cbs2chicago.com/local/
CTA.bus.Far.2.336905.html; Dana Kozlov and Kris
Habermehl, "Teen Dead, 4 Others Injured in Shoot-

ing on CTA Bus," http://cbs2chicago.com/local/shooting.CTA.bus.2.336925.html; Rummana Hussain, "Teen Killed on Bus Acted as Shield; Mother Grieves Loss of Ideal Son," *Chicago Sun-Times*, May 12, 2007, http://findarticles.com/p/articles/mi_qn4155/is_20070512/ai_n19112380.

10. You Want Me to Claim My Inheritance?

1. Christine E. Gudorf, *Journal of the Society of Christian Ethics,* Fall/Winter 2005 (Vol. 25, No. 2), p. 75; Stephen Goode, "How Faith Moves Across Mountains," *Insight Magazine,* April 13, 2004, electronically retrieved at http://findarticles.com/p/articles/mi_m1571/is_2004_April_13/ai_n6005699/pg_4.

2. Source: Personal interview with Art Fowler.

3. Pat Williams with Jim Denney, *How to Be Like Walt: Capturing the Disney Magic Every Day of Your Life* (Deerfield Beach, FL: Health Communications, Inc., 2004), pp. 23-54, passim.

4. Christopher Columbus and J. M. Cohen, *The Four Voyages: Being His Own Log-Book, Letters and Dispatches with Connecting Narratives* (New York: Penguin, 1969), pp. 33-36; The Applied History Research Group (The University of Calgary), "Christopher Columbus and the Spanish Empire," The European Voyages of Exploration website, retrieved at http://www.ucalgary.ca/applied_history/tutor/eurvoya/columbus.html.

11. You Want Me to Be a Runner to the City of Refuge?

1. John R. Wayland, *A Daily Passage Through Mark* (Houston, TX: Whitecaps Media, 2004), 126.

12. You Want Me to Tell the Story?

1. A. B. Earle, *Selected Sermon Illustrations from the Writings of Absalom Backas (A.B.) Earle and the Writings of J. Wilbur Chapman*, http://wesley.nnu .edu/wesleyctr/books/0101-0200/HDM0104.PDF.

About the Author

DR. MICHAEL YOUSSEF is the founding pastor of The Church of the Apostles in Atlanta. Dr. Youssef was born in Egypt and lived in Lebanon and Australia before becoming an American citizen in 1984. He holds degrees from Moore College in Sydney, Australia, and from Fuller University in California, as well as a PhD in social anthropology from Emory University. He and his wife reside in Atlanta and have four grown children and several grandchildren. You can learn more about him at www.apostles.org.